SHAD HELMSTETTER, PH.D.

Best-Selling Author of

What to Say When You Talk to Your Self

"A treasure you'll want to keep for a lifetime."

The

SECRET WORDS

of

SUCCESS

The Life-Changing Words
Successful People Use Most

① Purpose ② Direction ③ Meaning ④ Destiny
⑤ Future ⑥ Dream ⑦ Choices ⑧ Visualization
⑨ Commitment ⑩ Unlimited ⑪ Greatness

The words of Action
⑫ Targets ⑬ Goals ⑭ Plans ⑮ Motivation
⑯ Drive ⑰ Action ⑱ Work ⑲ Challenge
⑳ Discipline ㉑ Solution ㉒

Dealing with others ㉓ Caring ㉔ Encouragement ㉕
㉒ Relationships

The
Secret Words
of
Success

By Shad Helmstetter, Ph.D.

The Secret Words of Success

Published by Park Avenue Press
362 Gulf Breeze Pkwy., #104
Gulf Breeze, FL 32561

Helmstetter, Shad
The Secret Words of Success

ISBN: 978-1-7344982-1-9

Table of Contents

Introduction

The Success People

This is a book about the words of success——the special kind of success that most people would like to achieve, and the kind of success that can, with the right awareness and action, be achieved by anyone who chooses to do so.

'Success,' as we're using the term in these pages, does not refer to the person who measures his or her success only by money or power or position. The success we're referring to throughout this book is the kind of success that is made up of positive fulfillment—a daily sense of feeling in control, and a life that takes on the healthy glow of happiness and well-being—a sign that life is *working*.

The people who have attained this sense of happiness and well-being are an amazing group of individuals who are living among us right now. They are the *'success people.'*

The success people come from all walks of life—not just the rich or famous. They are the people who have trained their thoughts to help them live up to their potential, and who practice working at it every day. These success people are all around you. If you look for them, you can find them. You may already be one of them—or, if you're not one of the success people already, you can choose to become one.

This book identifies the key elements that make up this kind of success, the *words* that give the reader an actual success vocabulary, which, when put into practice, forms the foundation for creating enduring peace of mind and well-being—the hallmarks of practical, lasting success.

Chapter 1

Messages to the Brain

Each of us learns more than 20,000 words in our lifetime. The 'success person' focuses on fewer than 200 of them. By using these special words often, they become wired into the brain of the person who uses them, guiding the person in everything they do.

Hidden in plain sight, these are 'the secret words of success.'

*   *   *   *   *

This book gives you three key ingredients to help you create a positive attitude, peace of mind, and personal well-being. These ingredients are:

1) A brief overview of the science of self-talk and rewiring the brain.

2) The secret words that create the brain's success software.

3) Practical tools to help you move forward.

The Science of Self-Talk

For more than four decades, I have worked with people and with words—not just the meaning of words, but also their power and their hold on our lives. During those decades, I have written twenty-plus books, some of which, I am proud to say, have become popular world-wide.

However, I am most proud of my work in writing of another kind—the writing of passages of *positive self-talk.'* The self-talk passages I've written over the years consist of hundreds and hundreds—*thousands*—of messages that are designed to help you *talk to your brain*—to literally wire your brain to have more peace of mind, happiness, and success.

The reason I've spent so much time writing these self-talk 'messages to the brain' is that studies in the field of neuroscience show that because of the brain's neuroplasticity, the input our brain receives, including the words we use when we talk to ourselves, *physically* wires our brains with neural networks—*programs*—that direct and control our beliefs, our attitudes, and our actions.

This means that the words we use every day are incredibly important. Your self-talk— the *words* you say and think—are, through repetition, physically wiring your brain to create your future thoughts, set up your beliefs, choose your actions—and determine your success.

People who have learned to change their self-talk from *negative* to *positive* are more successful (they experience greater 'well-being'), than people whose minds are programmed to be negative. And yet, on their own, most people who are negative are often not aware of it, or even if they *are* aware of it, they find it difficult to do anything about it. Neuroscience explains why this is. It is based on *how* the brain gets wired:

People who think in the *'negative'* grow more neural networks in the *right* prefrontal cortex of their brains. *That's a part of the brain that stops you, limits solutions, causes you to run or to hide, or holds you back.*

This means that people who have been programmed to be negative have limited their brain's ability to find solutions and take the right action. The circuits in their brain that would have helped them find answers have been shut down. These people become cut off from their true potential, because their faulty wiring won't let them recognize the problem—let alone find the right solution.

But it is a much different picture for people who think in the *'positive.'* People who learn to think positively grow more neural networks in the *left* prefrontal cortex of their brains. That's a part of the brain that searches for alternatives, finds solutions, solves problems, and puts you into action.

The more connections you wire into this part of your brain, the more capable—and potentially, successful—you become. And all of this happens as a result of sending the right, repeated messages to the brain. As I've said elsewhere, the secret to success is *repetition, repetition, repetition.*

Self-Talk and the Secret Words of Success

Recognizing that it is through *repetition* that our brains become wired, a number of years ago I began to write and record audio recordings of self-talk messages that would help anyone, at any time, *re*wire their brain—and get it right.

My idea was that if we had, in our past, gotten programmed with the *wrong* messages, we could *re*program the brain by listening to recordings of the *right* messages. That proved to be correct.

The recordings made it possible for the listeners to experience the amount of repetition necessary for the positive new wiring to take place in their brains. The recordings were designed, through repeated, daily listening, to replace old, negative self-talk that hurts you, with new specially-worded self-talk that helps you.

What followed was years of writing and recording audio programs of positive self-talk. As a result, people all over the world now listen to those self-talk sessions every day. By listening to recorded sessions of self-talk, they find that rewiring their brains in the positive becomes a very simple process, much like learning a new language—by listening to it. With repeated listening, their brain records it, and gets it right.

Finding the Secret Words

Throughout those years, and continuing to this day, in order to write the most helpful self-talk messages possible, I had to find and use the words that would program the brain in the best possible way—the words that would create the strongest, clearest picture of successful thinking that the brain would understand, take action on, store, and keep for life. To get the self-talk messages right, finding the *right words* was the key.

Most people have an active vocabulary of an estimated 20,000 to 30,000 words. The breakthrough I discovered is that, of the more than 20,000 words we learn, the *success people* focus on a special subset of only a *few* of those words. They use these special words repeatedly, and they use them more often than other people use them.

That was a revelation to me: Out of a possible 20,000 or more words they could use, the success people *focus most on fewer than two hundred of them!*

This means that when they think or speak, the success people form their thinking with these words. They use them often, as part of their lives every day. They apply this 'success vocabulary' to everything they do—and, in turn, the words literally shape their core values, create their attitudes, and direct their success.

This goes far beyond typical positive thinking. Once wired in, the secret words of success create an entire *environment* of thinking and living in the most positive, yet practical and effective, way.

'Software' for your Brain

In my previous books, I have compared programming the brain to programming a computer—what you put in is what you get back out. The metaphor is accurate, and it applies directly to the secret words we will be discussing in this book. Your brain is the *hardware*, and the secret words of success are the *software*.

Anytime you learn anything, your brain creates new wiring based on the new information. In this instance, that's especially important; the result of learning these special words is that they become wired into your brain as new software—like a new *operating system*.

Because it's true that you only get back out what you put in, it's clear that the answer is to load your brain with the right software. If you want to live a positive, fulfilled life, the secret words of success are clearly an important part of the right software.

In the following pages, I have identified *101* of these special words. Along with the words themselves, I have added my definition of what each of the words means to the person who wants to use them to improve or get better at something or become more fulfilled in life.

The 101 words are not presented in order of importance (they're all important), but rather, they are grouped by categories that are identified by the chapters in which they appear. The words are also individually numbered for later reference.

It's More than the Words Themselves

What is especially interesting about these words is that, beyond just knowing the words, what is most important is the meaning or the *essence* of the words that becomes imbedded in the user's mind. That essence creates *a sense of 'being'*—living in the more positive, more productive mental environment the words bring to life.

So, it isn't just knowing the words that makes the difference; it isn't just the words themselves that have the power. It is the emotional environment, the *mental state* the words create. And it is that positive mental state which flourishes in the minds of the people who have wired the words into their brain and made them an essential part of who they are and how they think.

'Ordinary' Words— Extraordinary Power

When you first read these special words, they could appear to be nothing more than ordinary, everyday words. (Only a few of the words are longer than three syllables.) At first glance, any skeptic could say there's nothing new here—no magic—nothing special about them at all.

But keep reading. Watch what happens as the meanings of the words start to blend and weave together, as these simple, but powerful, words begin to form a special 'word tapestry'—a new picture of your own potential, and how you view your own world in your mind.

As you read the words and their meanings, pay special attention to the role each of them is playing in your life right now. Each time you read any of the words, you will be giving yourself a *self-assessment* of what is working in your life—and what isn't. That will tell you which of the words you want to highlight, or work on and emphasize in your own success vocabulary.

Special Self-Talk for the Secret Words

Along with identifying the special words, I have also included examples of how the words are used in actual phrases of self-talk—the kind of self-talk passages I've written and recorded to help people rewire their brains with a more successful kind of thinking.

Self-talk passages are best internalized by repeated listening to them over several weeks. However, the self-talk phrases I've written for each of the special words here, even if you're only reading them, will familiarize you with the kinds of messages that have proven to be the most effective.

One Step at a Time

A note of caution: As you read the secret words and think about what each of them means to you personally, it is possible to be overwhelmed by the quantity of the words, and also by the immediate desire to make each of them important, right now, in your own life.

But give this time. Don't try to adopt or master all the words at once. You might want to try reading only a chapter—or a few of the secret words from that chapter—at a time, allowing yourself a chance to apply those words before you move on.

Or, you may want to initially read through the entire book to get a feel for the breadth and depth of the words, and then read the book again, more slowly, using the tools (such as the workbook that goes along with this book), to help you dig deeper and master the words that are most important to you.

The goal is not to attain a 'perfect' understanding of all of the words, or even to apply them perfectly. (We can never be perfect.) Instead of expecting perfection in using the words, the goal should be that, with practice, you not only become more mindful of the words, but you also find yourself applying them in ways that are truly meaningful to your life.

Tools You Can Use

To assist you in making these words your own, in the final chapter of the book, Chapter 12, I've included several helpful tools you can download and use at no cost. One of these tools is the *"The Secret Words Workbook,"* created specifically to go along with the book you're reading.

Another tool I've included is a self-coaching program called *"Six Weeks to Success"* that you can download and use at home. In addition, there is a link that lets you download my personal goal-setting form, which is easy to use and has helped thousands of people set and track their goals.

You can also download the *'The Secret Words'* wall poster, which lists all of the words together, that you can print out and post on the wall to keep the words in front of you. In addition, I've included, below, the link for listening to the recorded self-talk audio sessions.* If you'd like to make the secret words a part of your life, all of these tools will help.

*   *   *   *   *   *

Here, then, are my choices of the words the success people use that will do the most to create success and well-being in your own life. Get to know these words. Use them often; wire them into your brain and make them a part of your life. When you do, you will own them forever.

* To listen to recorded self-talk audio sessions, go to: www.selftalkplus.com.

Chapter 2

The Secret Words for
Getting Started

As you read each of the secret words in this chapter, think of the power each of the words has, and the role each of them plays in your own life now, as you move forward on your journey.

The success people who already have this sense of 'well-being' I spoke about—those who have already imbedded the messages of the words into their thinking—are fortunate. Even if they didn't actively try to 'program in' the words and the meanings themselves, their experiences or their upbringing gave them the right words—and wired the words into their brain *for* them.

Fortunately, if you know the right words, you can do that for yourself. With practice and repetition, you can have the same words working for you.

To get started, we will focus in this chapter on the special words success people use to *set their direction* and *stay on course*. We'll start with the word ***purpose***.

1. Purpose

This is a word that should precede any direction you set in your life.

Purpose often gets confused with the 'why' that people express when they're working at reaching a goal. Your 'why' gives you a reason for doing something that is important to you. But your *purpose* defines why you have the 'why' in the first place.

Your purpose is bigger than your 'why.' Your reason for wanting to earn more money may be to enroll your child in a better school. That's your 'why.' But your purpose for doing that is bigger than the choice of the school; it may be to help your child grow up to improve the world—or something else that's more important than any of the *whys* along the way.

True purpose is long-term. It is your overarching goal in life—the most distant target at which you're aiming your arrow. Your *purpose* is your clearest, long-range, most-focused understanding of why you are here in the first place.

*   *   *

*Why **purpose** matters:*

The opposite of having a mindset of *purpose* is going through your life with no life-defining focus. Living *without* purpose keeps you in a constant state of wondering what it's all for. Living *with* a highly defined purpose is one of the primary contributors to personal fulfillment. If you can identify your purpose clearly enough, it will set the tone for the important focus of your life.

*   *   *

Using **purpose** in a phrase of positive self-talk:

"I have purpose in my life, and it is greater than the day-to-day responsibilities I deal with along the way. I have a greater purpose, a greater value, and a greater responsibility than all of those. I have purpose in my life."

2. Direction

I've never met a success person who was aimless. In fact, the clearer someone's direction, the better they do. They make their moments count, because they know where they're going, and they know what to do next.

I've known people who work very hard, and struggle endlessly, but never get anywhere—because they have no clear idea where they want to go or how to get there. They have no direction. Either they never learned, or they forgot, that setting their direction, and knowing exactly what it is, is up to them. (Ultimately, choosing our own direction is up to each of us.)

The more you are consciously aware of your direction, the better the chance you'll get where you want to go. That may seem so apparent it could be a cliche'—but look around you. Ask yourself which of the people you know have a crystal-clear picture of their direction in life. And then, ask the same question of yourself.

* * *

*Why **direction** matters:*

The opposite mindset of having *direction* is to be aimless, or guided by chance. With the difficulties and tragedies that are a normal part of life, leaving your direction up to the odds of chance has little hope of working. With a mindset of purposeful *direction,* you immediately increase the probability of following a better track, being happier, and living closer to your true potential.

* * *

Using **direction** in a phrase of positive self-talk:

"I have direction in my life. I make sure I have a clear picture of where I'm going, and how to get there. Because I know my direction, I'm playing the leading role in creating my own future."

3. Meaning

Like a life without *purpose*, a life without *meaning* never works well. It could be said that if you spent most of your life searching for meaning, and then, after finding it, you spent the rest of your life *living* your meaning, you would have a successful life.

The idea of having meaning in your life is important, because it says you are more than a temporary mortal being with no higher value—that there is meaning in your being here, a reason you were born in the first place.

When people aren't certain what their meaning in life is, I've recommended that, to begin the quest of finding it, each morning for the next thirty days—or as long as it takes—they ask themselves the question *"What is my meaning?"* The more you focus on the question, the closer you will come to finding your answer.

* * *

*Why **meaning** matters:*

The opposite mindset of having a life of meaning creates a void in your spirit that cannot be filled by anything else. Not having meaning leaves you questioning and unfulfilled—*being* here, but not knowing why. Having meaning not only tells you why you are here; but it also keeps you mindful of living up to the person you came here to be.

*   *   *

Using **meaning** in a phrase of positive self-talk:

"I have meaning in my life. I have meaning and purpose and value and worth. I am so much more than my body and mind alone, and there is a reason I am here. Finding— and living—my meaning is an important goal in my life."

4. Destiny

Many people feel that their destiny, their ultimate future, is not up to them. They see the future as written in the stars, or the result of the whims of fate. Most success people, however, take the notion of *kismet* out of the word destiny. To them, it is their *focus*—not their *fate*—that guides them.

That makes a lot of sense. It would be easy to see that if you did little or nothing to direct your own course in life—and just hoped for the best—you would be adrift, and your direction in life would be left up to the mindless winds of chance.

Success people who take the time and expend the effort to have control over their own lives—with a healthy dose of the right balance in all things—are also the most fulfilled. Which, they would tell you, was their *destiny*.

* * *

*Why **destiny** matters:*

Not having a sense of personal destiny can cause you to imagine yourself as being less important than you were born to be. With a mindset that makes you aware of your own destiny, you are able to see your greater worth, and appreciate how valuable you truly are. It reminds you of your duty to live up to your potential, and it assures you there is a reason you are here.

* * *

Using **destiny** in a phrase of positive self-talk:

"I choose to play the primary role in the creation of my own destiny. I understand that life itself has its rules, and sets its own course. But I take full responsibility for the direction and the outcome of my own life."

5. Future

Success people make it a point to live in the present—but they also focus on their future. The reason they spend time focusing on the future is because they know that they, like you, are creating their tomorrows, today. For you, that places a lot of importance on what you're doing now—because whatever you're thinking or doing, it is, each day, shaping your future.

The more you take control of creating your own future, the more familiar and the more possible it becomes. There will always be unknowns in your future, but the more time you spend creating a clear, well-thought-out path to getting there, the better the chance you'll have of creating the future of your choice.

*   *   *

*Why **future** matters:*
The opposite of a positive future mindset is a feeling of helplessness—an inability to affect the outcome. If there is no positive future you can see—or no future you feel you

are a part of creating—it's easy to give in to despondency, and begin to feel that you don't count. A success person would tell you: having a *future* mindset is the beginning of being in control of your life—and creating a future that works.

*   *   *

Using **future** in a phrase of positive self-talk:

"I choose to build a future that works! So, although I learn from my past, and have my feet firmly grounded in the present, I do everything I need to do today, to create the future I choose to have tomorrow."

6. Dream

While it's always good to have your feet on solid ground, you go almost nowhere unless you're willing to dream—the kind of dreaming you do when you're fully awake. And although dreaming without *doing* leads to a life of unfulfilled wishes, dreaming plus *action* can create a life of personal fulfillment and accomplishment.

If you're experienced at 'productive dreaming,' you already know that this kind of dreaming can create amazing things, and open incredible doors for you. If you're not practiced at productive dreaming, you should know that it is a skill—something that can be learned and can be improved with practice.

When was the last time you dreamed— *really dreamed?* The kind of dreaming where you took the limits off and let your mind soar completely free? It's so easy to get into the groove (or rut) of everyday living, that 'normal' becomes 'complacency.' We forget how *un*limited we really are, and what we could be doing with our lives if we stopped being our robot selves and really dreamed once again.

This is a case in which we can learn from children. From a very young age, children dream of the most amazing things, and they continue to do so until they learn—taught by indifferent or disillusioned adults—to be practical, and to stop dreaming.

But children have it right. Of course, part of growing up is learning to be practical. But having the courage to continue to dream, at *any* age, often separates the truly fulfilled person from the person who 'lives,' but never does anything more than exist while they're here.

So, in the most caring way, I will ask the question again: When is the last time you dreamed—*really dreamed?*

* * *

*Why **dream** matters:*
If you do not *dream*, you set yourself up to live a life of passive acceptance, tolerating the status quo—even when the status quo

isn't working. By allowing yourself to dream, life takes on a positive glow—a new perspective with a different feel. With a mindset of dreaming, you are able to look forward to the next sunrise; your enthusiasm for tomorrow changes from wishing for what *could* have been—to creating what *will* be.

* * *

Using ***dream*** in a phrase of positive self-talk:

"I will never stop dreaming. I have learned how to dream in the most positive and productive way. And because I do, there are always doors of creativity and opportunity that open in front of me."

7. Choices

Choices is one of the most important words in the vocabulary of the success people. And making good choices makes the difference between achieving happiness and well-being, or putting up with something less.

This is one of the words on our list that initiates action. Having *choices* means that you have the option of being in control of your life—everything from the smallest details of your day, to the future you have in front of you. It is the recognition of the need to make the right choices, and then making those choices—*and acting on them*—that often sets successful people apart from the less successful.

How much do you want to earn? How much do you want to weigh? Where do you want to live? How do you want to spend your time? Who do you want to spend your time with? What do you want to talk about? What hobbies do you want to focus on most? What will you do with an hour of free time that you found? What time do you want to get up in the morning? What is the last thing you will think about before you go to sleep tonight?

Each of us makes dozens of choices in a day—most of which we don't even know we're making. And many of those choices, no matter how seemingly insignificant they may be at the time, can have a profound influence on not only future events, but have consequences in the lives of people we don't even know.

Success people become super-aware that their day is made up of making those choices. And one of the reasons they end up being successful is because they take personal responsibility for getting their choices right. They know what they want, and they make conscious choices that help them get there.

*　*　*

*Why **'choices'** matters:*
The opposite mindset of making good choices is allowing *chance* to make your choices for you—and chance makes poor choices. When you have a mindset of making choices for yourself, you take back ownership

of your right to choose—and that includes choosing your happiness, your peace of mind, and your successes in life.

*   *   *

Using **choices** in a phrase of positive self-talk:

"I make good choices. I am consciously aware of the choices I make every day—from the smallest choices I make, to the major choices that set the direction of my life. In every moment, every opportunity, every day, I make good choices."

8. Visualization

A practice that is common to all success people is the practice of *visualization*.

Visualization has been a mainstay of the personal growth movement since it began. It is the practice of seeing, in your mind, any goal in its finished form—in advance.

The more you visualize your completed goal in your mind, the clearer your picture of the future happening becomes, and the stronger you wire a picture of the completed goal into your brain. When you do this, your chances of reaching that goal increase dramatically.

This is because the clearer and more detailed the picture you give to your brain, the easier it is for your brain to act on it. If the picture is clear enough, your brain will bring its mass of hidden programs to bear to help you bring the picture you see into actual reality. The more you see it, the more your brain will help you create it in your life.

As a result, visualization is one of the first and most frequent tools success people use when they start the process of moving from *idea,* to *plan,* to *action.* They visualize—again and again—not only the completed goal, but also each step of the process along the way.

As an example from my own life, for years, each of the books I've written has started with an early idea—the concept of the book—and also a *picture* of the cover of the completed book that I visualized in my mind. To complete the picture, I have often created a life-like mock-up of the book, with printed, full-color covers, that appear in every way to be the finished book.

Holding what appears to be the 'completed' book in my hands—even before the book is written—imprints an indelible picture of that book in my mind. Once the picture is clearly imprinted in my mind, my own brain becomes a positive motivator, coaching me onward to work hard, write the book, and complete the goal.

Most of us, with practice, can create marvelously detailed pictures in our minds. Since your brain is designed to act on the directions you give it, you might as well create good, clear, detailed pictures of what you would like to have in your future. When, with repetition, you wire those pictures into your brain, your brain will help you make it happen.

Visualization is the key to doing that.

*　*　*

*Why **visualization** matters:*
The opposite of a visualization mindset condemns you to a life of perpetual wishing and hoping—but without the attainment that could have been yours, had you been able to *see* it clearly—in advance. Visualizing opens your eyes to the possibilities that could become real, and allows your mind first to *see* them—and then to help you *create* them.

*　*　*

Using *visualization* in a phrase of positive self-talk:

"I practice active visualization. I see clear, detailed pictures of my goals and my future in my mind. The more I visualize them, the more I make those pictures come true."

9. Commitment

Commitment is a powerful secret word of success. One reason is that a *commitment* is an *agreement* with yourself—and success people make a habit of keeping their agreements.

Another reason commitment is important to success people is that without the personal sacrifice of commitment there is no true appreciation of attainment. True success is *earned*; it is never given to you. And without your commitment driving you forward, there may be little chance of achieving it—or appreciating the success, once it is yours.

Commitment is an agreement made with determination. It is an emotional drive. So, it is something that comes mostly from the *heart*, rather than from the intellect.

Real commitment is also a choice you have to make personally; it's a choice that no one else can make *for* you. Whether it is the choice of taking the new job or going back to school or setting a goal and starting a gym membership, it is *your* commitment that will set into motion a part of the direction of the next days or months or years of your life.

Success people learn to ask themselves the question: *Is this a commitment?* Ask yourself that question the next time a new idea or opportunity comes up that requires your personal time or involvement, or you're confronted with anything that gives you the option of making a personal commitment.

When you make a *commitment*—a real, heart-felt, personal commitment—and act on it, you are putting into motion a major step toward a future result.

*   *   *

*Why **commitment** matters:*
The opposite of a mindset of commitment is to live without placing value on your goals. It allows a lack of conviction to bury good intentions before they are born. A mindset of *commitment* is the inner spirit and dedication that brings them to life.

*   *   *

Using **commitment** in a phrase of positive self-talk:

"I know that my commitment is an agreement with myself—and I always keep my agreements. My commitments are also the bedrock of my goals, and when I commit, I make them happen."

10. Unlimited

Success people accept fewer limitations than other people accept. That's because they look at life in a more *unlimited* way. Because they are not bound or shackled by what cannot be done, their creativity takes hold, and new ideas come to life. History is full of endless examples of people who helped change the world, because they looked at life in an unlimited way.

Thinking about things in an unlimited way doesn't mean you have to ignore the boundaries of reality, or pretend you can do the impossible. But it does mean you're willing to stretch those boundaries to their limits, and think beyond the normal fences of an everyday mind.

It means you're willing to let your mind soar, and open up to the possibilities that are certain to be there—but only if you're willing to push your mind beyond the ordinary, and allow your thoughts, in that moment, to be *unlimited*.

* * *

*Why **unlimited** matters:*

A mindset that does not include the concept of *unlimited*, is a mindset that accepts limitations before they have had a chance to be overcome. An *unlimited* mindset sees the world in an open, infinitely creative way. To the unlimited mindset, the possibilities are endless. This is the mindset that is always ready to say *"I can!"*—before it says *"I can't."*

*   *   *

Using **unlimited** in a phrase of positive self-talk, reworded here from a quote I penned some forty years ago, when I first wrote about self-talk:

"I am everything that is, my thoughts, my life, my dreams come true. I am everything I choose to be. I am as unlimited as the endless universe."

11. Greatness

One of my favorite passages of self-talk begins with the words, *"Greatness begins in the minds of the great."*

Greatness means the achievement of a high level of quality, character, and accomplishment. It's a worthy aspiration, because striving for greatness encourages you to live up to your best. It doesn't mean you ignore your faults and failings; it means you work to overcome them and rise above them.

There are many ways to experience greatness. There can be greatness in high achievement, but there can also be greatness in humility, or steadfastness, or caring for others.

Some people might think that wanting any kind of greatness is reaching for the sky. But when you consider the alternative, why would you want to reach for anything less?

* * *

*Why **greatness** matters:*

Without having a mindset of *greatness*, you can never be great. The opposite of a mindset of greatness is low self-esteem (your self-created picture of yourself). Without a belief in your own potential greatness, you limit yourself to being a less capable, less qualified, *less-than-great* version of you. *With* a mindset of greatness, you're willing to do what it takes to be capable, qualified, and the greatest possible version of yourself.

*   *   *

Using **greatness** in a phrase of positive self-talk:

"I choose to do everything I can do to live up to my best. For me, striving for greatness means that I have made the decision to live a positive and exceptional life in every way I can. And every day, that's what I do."

Chapter 3

The Secret Words for
Putting Yourself into Action

Imagine for a moment, that there were *two* of you. *One* of you learned the secret words, practiced them, internalized them— *owned them*—and made them a part of your daily life. The *other* you did not learn or practice the words, and saw them only as an interesting list, but nothing more. If you had to choose, which of you would you vote for, to win in life? In every case, I would vote for *the you that owns the words.*

In the previous chapter, we covered words that set your direction, so you know your purpose, and you know *why* you're going to do what you do next. In this chapter, we look into the words that help you choose the target, set the goal, take action, stay with it, and get things done.

The success people, those among us whose lives are working well, seldom have to be coaxed into action—they're already there. They have wired their brains to keep them motivated and moving. The words in this chapter make it immediately clear how this happens, and how you can do it for yourself. Once the words are wired into your brain, they create a complete *environment* of positive activity in your mind. And that creates positive activity in your day.

Notice how each of the words in this chapter, even the first time you read them, work together to 'up' your level of interest in choosing your targets, taking action, and getting things done. Imagine that happening to an even greater degree after a few weeks of wiring the words in, and owning them!

We'll begin with the secret word that perfectly sets you up for taking action. That word is *'target.'*

12. Target

Unless you identify your targets and know what they are, you can spend a lot of time missing them. (Interestingly, the original use of the word *'sin'* is an archery term, meaning *'to miss the target.'*)

All of our targets should be obvious—and yet we so easily miss them. That's often because we're not looking for them. As a person who trains life coaches, and is also an avid, long-distance archer, I think about targets a lot, and how incredibly important they are to each of us. But you don't have to be an Olympic archer to recognize the importance of targets in your life.

For the person who wants to do his or her best, *target* is a word that is a perfect metaphor. The target is your goal, and the arrow is your action. It is because of that metaphor—aiming at something and hitting the mark with the right action—that success people use this word a lot.

Whether they are aware of them or not, everyone has targets. (Some targets are positive; some are not.) Your own targets are either clear and strong—and obvious to you—or they can be vague and hidden. The difference with success people is that they have learned to clearly identify their targets—so that none of them are hidden. They know exactly what they're aiming at. They know what to focus on, and what to spend their time on.

How are your targets? Ask yourself the questions: *"What are my top three targets right now?"* and *"What are the seven most important targets in my life?"* If you can come up with even a few answers to those questions, you're doing well.

* * *

*Why **target** matters:*
Having a mindset that doesn't create targets causes you to drift in the wind. It is a mindset that doesn't clearly see the difference between vague ideas and solid goals. When you have a *target mindset,* you have a center point—a bullseye—that you can see and focus on. With practice, you are very likely to hit your mark.

*   *   *

Using **target** in a phrase of positive self-talk:

"I am good at identifying my targets, hitting my targets, and reaching my goals. I know every important target I have in my life. With each target that is important to me, I know it, I see it, I take aim, and I make sure the arrow of my activity reaches its mark."

13. Goals

Success people are very serious about setting goals. The reason for this is that the setting of a goal is the first action step in bringing an idea to life; the goal initiates the action.

A goal, if you don't write it down, is little more than a wish. You may have a dream, but it is the moment you set the goal—and actually *write it down* on paper—that your goal begins to move from dream to reality.

The reason consciously focusing on your goals is so helpful is that the process of setting and reviewing goals actually wires the goals into your brain—and subconsciously alerts your brain to take action on them!

Some people have trouble taking the time to write out their goals and review them daily—or even weekly—because they have never developed the habit of doing so. But it is one of the most important habits you can create, and something people who want to be successful practice doing.

For an easy, but very effective way to write and track your goals, you can download copies of the simple goal-setting form I personally use at:

www.thesecretwordsofsuccess.com/tools

* * *

*Why **'goals'** matters:*

The opposite of a *goals mindset* is one that leaves the details of your life up to chance— *'whatever will be will be.'* Like others of the secret words, being a *goal-setter* is about taking responsibility for everything that makes up your journey. Having a goals mindset not only makes setting goals a serious habit, but it also keeps you mindful of how much control you really *do* have in determining what happens next.

* * *

Using *goals* in a phrase of positive self-talk:

"I am good at setting and reaching goals. I choose my goals, I write them down, I review them regularly, I take action, and I reach my goals."

14. Plan

Plan is an action word that identifies the rest of the action steps you're going to take. Having a *plan* is actually one of the easiest of the secret word concepts to put into practice. That's fortunate because, for success people, having a *plan* is an essential working part of their lives.

With a plan, you have a strategy. *Without* a plan, you're winging it, and you have nothing to rely on but serendipity or luck. If you don't have a written plan, don't blame the world for your idea not working.

Every truly successful person has a plan for each of the important new steps they take. They may start off with a whim, or a single creative thought, but if they end up being successful, somewhere along the way they began to plan.

No matter how much you believe in fate or your divine destiny, back it up with a *plan*. (Harry Potter started his life on a cocktail napkin in a train station in England.) The success of any endeavor begins with the first ideas of your creative thoughts—but it is brought to life by your *plan.*

* * *

*Why **plan** matters:*
The opposite of a *plan* is *accident* or *chaos.* The lack of specific objectives, with no detailed action steps and no targeted completion dates, can doom your best intentions to failure. A good plan tells you *who, what, where, how,* and *when*—so you know where you're starting from, you know where you're going, and you know what to do next. A good plan is a beautiful thing. It is the map that leads to the treasure.

* * *

Using **plan** in a phrase of positive self-talk:

"I write clear, detailed plans, and I review them often. When I want to achieve a goal, no matter what it is, I make sure I have a plan to reach the goal. Following my plan brings my goal to life."

15. Motivation

Success people love the word *motivation*. And to them, the most important kind of motivation is *self*-motivation, which means *'putting yourself into motion.'* Doing that, affirms that you are responsible for your own successes. Your personal motivation—and therefore, your success—is up to you.

The success people are right about this. It has been my experience that you cannot motivate someone *else*—beyond getting them to take action for brief periods of time. You can have someone encourage you or push you, like the coach who is trying to get you moving. But the only *real* motivation, the kind that lasts, comes from *within*. The things that create your motivation—your dream, your positive self-talk, your determination, your belief in the value of your quest—are what will keep you moving when the coach goes home.

* * *

*Why **motivation** matters:*

The opposite of a motivation mindset is procrastination, lethargy and inactivity. An unmotivated mindset is also a *habit*—so doing nothing ends up being the default thing to do. A motivation mindset, one that fills you with enthusiasm for taking action and puts you into focused motion, is the mindset that makes the difference between winning the race—or staying home.

* * *

Using **motivation** in a phrase of positive self-talk:

"My motivation is important to me. I make sure I have the daily motivation I need to put myself into motion, take action, tackle the task, see it through, and have motivation to spare."

16. Drive

Personal *drive* (as a noun) is a valuable asset to have, and it's easy to see why drive is something active success people make sure they have plenty of. Drive is made up of *interest, focus, determination, action, energy,* and *endurance*—so it's a small word with a lot of meaning built into it. (If you're ever filling out a resume, be sure to place the word *"Drive"* near the top of your list of personal attributes.)

You may have natural drive, as a part of your emotional and energetic makeup. However, if drive doesn't come naturally to you, you can create it by increasing your interest and your focus—the amount of enthusiasm and attention you invest in a goal. Either way, you'll almost always accomplish more *with* drive than without it.

If you were to make a list of truly great achievements, you will find that *none* of them was accomplished without someone, somewhere along the way, having *drive*.

*   *   *

*Why **drive** matters:*

The opposite of a drive mindset is an attitude of idle indifference. That can happen either out of habit, or when you don't see the value in taking action. Having a *drive mindset* tells you that what you're doing counts—and what you do makes a difference—so you go for it, get things done, and feel great about yourself. You should. You deserve it. You have drive.

* * *

Using **drive** in a phrase of positive self-talk:

"I choose to create enthusiasm and drive for anything I do that is important to me. When I have something I truly want to do, I make sure I have the drive I need to make it happen and see it through."

17. Action

Ultimately, *action* is the key to most successful endeavors. For success people, *action* is the vital step of putting yourself into motion—and getting something done. Action is best achieved by getting out of bed, or making the phone call, or defining your plan and acting on it, or doing something you need to do, or doing anything productive that puts your brain and your life into motion.

Action is especially important to our list of the secret words of success, because it is what brings many of them to life. In fact, many of the secret words are effective precisely *because* of the action they inspire.

Not taking action, when action is required (procrastination or avoidance), is a habit that success people have learned to overcome. Taking action is also a habit, and it is best learned by refusing to put off doing anything that needs to be done. The more you immediately put yourself into action when action is called for, the more natural and automatic the 'action habit' becomes.

Most important to the success person is the habit of taking action when an idea requires momentum to make it work. Without action, nothing of value is accomplished. With the right plan to follow, taking action is the key step to achieving *anything*.

* * *

*Why **action** matters:*
The opposite of an action mindset is *stasis*—the critical resting point between *stop* and *go*. People who are not action-oriented have trouble achieving anything of merit. People who have learned to make action their standard mindset have learned that *action* and *accomplishment* go hand in hand.

* * *

Using *action* in a phrase of positive self-talk:

"I have created the habit of taking action. Anytime action is required, I take action. And when I have a goal I want to reach, instead of waiting, hoping, or wishing—I take action, and I get things done."

18. Effort

The positive meaning of effort is "effective work." Effort is something you choose to give to doing something worthwhile. *Without* your effort, it probably won't work. *With* your effort—sometimes a lot of it—you have a much better chance of succeeding. If you want to know how important a goal is to you, ask yourself the question *"How much effort am I willing to put into reaching this goal?"*

When you use the word 'effort,' always see it in its most positive form. Instead of a weighty obligation, practice seeing effort as something you can add at any time to make things work.

There is truth to the words, *"The greater your effort, the greater your success."* When you make the choice to put your effort into any worthwhile goal, you're making the choice to make it work.

* * *

*Why **effort** matters:*

A mindset that tolerates a lack of effort is doomed to mediocrity, and usually, failure. A mindset that sees *effort* as a positive tool for achievement, changes that; a goal with effort is a dream with heart.

*   *   *

Using **effort** in a phrase of positive self-talk:

"I am good at reaching my goals. I consciously choose to add the strength of my personal effort to accomplishing anything that is important to me."

19. Work

I personally learned, some years ago, to *like* the word *'work.'* That's because, being unable to find any way around having to perform it, I decided to change the *meaning* of the word in my mind. So I did. I changed the word 'work' from meaning something difficult, or something to be avoided, or something that was hard and tiring—to something more positive.

My definition, now, recognizes work for the productive blessing that it is. Work is: *'Something you get to do to accomplish your goals.'*

If you struggle with this one, try redefining the word 'work' in your own mind, and you may be pleasantly surprised at the result.

* * *

*Why **work** matters:*
The opposite of a positive work mindset is a lack of responsibility for getting things done. It presupposes that effort and exertion

are by nature something to be avoided. Without a positive work mindset, what is avoided most is success.

*   *   *

Using **work** in a phrase of positive self-talk:

"I see 'work' as a positive. It is a blessing in so many ways! Work helps me reach my goals, gives me a chance to excel, and builds my self-esteem. It is because of the work I gladly do, that I am able to accomplish so much."

20. Challenge

There is nothing that creates more growth in our lives than *challenge*. Without difficulty, without problems, without challenges to motivate us, to push us forward, we never find our strength, and we achieve little of value.

It is challenge that makes almost all good things worthwhile. It is challenge that forces us to grow our muscles and our brain. Without challenge, we would be weak and undeveloped. But with challenge, we grow stronger and smarter.

It makes sense, then, to see challenge not as something to be avoided, but rather as something that is a natural part of moving forward—and getting better.

* * *

*Why **challenge** matters:*
Without a mindset that embraces positive challenge, instead of confronting problems, dealing with them and learning from them, it is easy to live in fear and avoidance. With a

positive challenge mindset, fear turns into preparedness, and avoidance turns into action —and that turns into the potential for accomplishment.

*   *   *

Using *challenge* in a phrase of positive self-talk:

"I know that challenge is an important part of my growth. When I meet a challenge of any kind, I deal with it, I overcome it, and I learn from it. I am good at dealing with challenges."

21. Discipline

There are two definitions that apply, here, to the word *discipline*. One is *"to make a disciple of."* That's a good way to look at discipline when you're raising children.

The other definition is about *self-discipline*—the kind of discipline which tells you that you are firmly in control of your time, your attitude, your actions, your output, and your accomplishments. If discipline were scored on a 1 to 10 scale, with 10 being the best, you probably already know what your own discipline score would be.

If, like other successful people, you want to make sure your discipline is strong, it will help you to know which areas of discipline you score high in, and which areas need improvement. Are you on time? Do you schedule your tasks? Do you do everything you need to do when you need to do it? Do you have any habits that work against you? In what areas are you *most* disciplined? In what areas are you *least* disciplined?

Everyone who wants to live up to their best, learns that discipline is one thing they must have if they want to reach their goals. That makes discipline a focus that is essential.

* * *

*Why **discipline** matters:*
To live without a mindset of discipline is to live without knowing what will work, and what's coming next—because there is no one at the helm. With a mindset of *discipline*, not only do you have more control, you also create less stress, reduce the number of failures, increase the number of successes, and add to your personal fulfillment.

* * *

Using ***discipline*** in a phrase of positive self-talk:

"I make sure I have the discipline I need to reach any objective I set. I am organized, disciplined, and in control of my life."

22. Solution

Many of our greatest leaps forward, and most of the conveniences and tools of life we now have, happened only because someone was faced with a problem and ended up creating a solution. To the success person, when there is a *problem*, finding a *solution* is always the goal.

To the success person, problems are not about fear or uncertainty; recognizing the problem is just the first step to finding a solution. Since you can neither live nor grow without having to face and overcome problems—sometimes a lot of them—having a mindset that helps you focus on finding solutions is a healthy mindset to have.

Interestingly, because of the way the human brain becomes wired, the brain of the person who thinks in the *positive* is wired to find more *solutions* than the person who thinks in the negative.

* * *

*Why **solution** matters:*

The opposite of a solution-oriented mindset is perpetual quandary—being constantly unsure about what to do next. People who do not automatically and methodically search for solutions to problems are destined to live lives of fear and uncertainty. The good news is that with a solution mindset, the solutions you are seeking—when you look for them—are often right in front of you.

* * *

Using **solution** in a phrase of positive self-talk:

"When I face a problem of any kind, the first thing I do is to identify the steps that will lead to the best solution. I am practical and realistic, and I always know there is a solution waiting to be found, for any problem I face."

Chapter 4

The Secret Words for
Dealing with Others

The way we feel about others, and deal with them, affects almost everything in our lives. The special words in this chapter will increase your awareness of not only how you feel about the people around you, but also who you are as an individual.

Some people never think about what is behind their relationships. They never ask themselves the questions, *"How do I see other people? How to I feel about them? How do I see myself?"* and *"How can I do better?"* Knowing the answers to those questions directly affects your self-esteem, your happiness, and your sense of well-being—all essential ingredients if you want to be successful.

The secret words in this chapter will give you some of the answers. If you begin to use these words frequently, as you shape your own identity in the most positive way, you should see your relationships with others grow—and your relationship with *yourself* getting better than ever.

NOTE: To download the free user tools—*The Secret Words Workbook, The Secret Words Poster, Six Weeks to Success* home coaching program, and *Personal Goal-Setting Forms*—see Chapter 12, or go to:
www.thesecretwordsofsuccess.com/tools

---

23. Relationships

We are amazingly dependent on our relationships. They are a major part of our lives. And yet, we can often neither perfect them—nor do without them. Since your relationships *will* affect your successes in almost anything, what magic should you do to make your relationships work for you?

Dozens of books by brilliant authors have been written to address this one question: *What should you do to make your relationships work?* My personal answer is so simple that it could be overlooked: If you want to make your relationships work, live each day as close to the *Golden Rule* as you possibly can: *"Do unto others as you would have them do unto you."*

That solution sounds simple, but it works. Do your best to live every day with the kind of self-agreed-upon rules of success we're talking about in this book—the rules of *honesty, integrity, character, caring, compassion, sharing, belief, harmony, encouragement,* and *commitment.* With those guidelines directing your life, you are likely to have relationships that work.

*   *   *

Why **'relationships'** *matters:*
Having a *negative* mindset on relationships is usually the result of negative mental programs—created when problems with past relationships caused the person to protect themselves from pain or loss or emotional duress. Choosing to have a *positive* relationship mindset allows you to see relationships as being *positive, healthy,* and *highly worthwhile*—which is the beginning of any good relationship.

*   *   *

Using **relationships** in a phrase of positive self-talk:

"I have wonderful relationships! I honor, respect, listen to, believe in, and encourage the people I know in my life. I am a quality person, and I choose to make all of my relationships quality relationships."

24. Caring

Caring is an essential part of a worthwhile life. Caring identifies how each of us relates to the condition of others. It is a word that is a part of our lives from our mother's first feelings toward us to the thoughts we think when someone we love passes on. Throughout our lives, there are an infinite number of opportunities to care.

Caring requires you to have *empathy, consideration, understanding,* and *compassion.* No one who fails to care about others ends up living a life that is completely fulfilled. Caring is one of the most important parts of a worthwhile life. There is no true quality of life without it.

*   *   *

*Why **caring** matters:*
The opposite of a mindset of caring is indifference or lack of empathy. If you don't consciously *care,* you miss out on many of those things in life that bring joy, appreciation, a sense of community, and fulfillment—exactly the kinds of things you

create by having a mindset of caring. When you care, you and the other person both win.

*   *   *

Using **caring** in a phrase of positive self-talk:

"I care. I make sure I take the time to look around me, see the needs that are there, do what I need to do to help, and take the time to care."

25. Encouragement

Encouragement is the practice of strengthening someone by giving them courage. Success people are good at this. They practice telling others, *"You've got it,"* *"You can do this,"* and, *"I believe in you."*

What is most remarkable about giving encouragement to someone is that it is a gift you can give that has no *cost*. When you give encouragement, instead of taking something *from* you, it *gives* you, the giver, more of the same.

Success people also get good at giving themselves encouragement in their own self-talk when they say, *"I've got it,"* *"I can do this,"* and *"I believe in myself."* The more you say those words, the truer they become.

Courage is something everyone needs to have just to get through life. Fortunately, encouragement is something you can create more of—anytime you choose to do so.

*   *   *

Why **encouragement** *matters:*

The opposite of an encouragement mindset manifests itself as a lack of consideration for others. With an encouragement mindset, you do more good for yourself—and you do a great deal to uplift the people around you.

*   *   *

Using **encouragement** in a phrase of positive self-talk:

"I always encourage others, and I always encourage myself. The more encouragement I give, and the more I help others do better, the more courage I have to share."

26. Trust

Trust is a way of putting courage and belief into practice. It is when you have the courage to trust yourself that you can have real trust in others.

Having trust and extending it to others is important, because throughout our lives we need a sense of stability—we need to know that some things are reliable, that we can count on them—and trust gives us that.

Choosing to trust doesn't mean you're always certain of the results. It means you have assessed the odds, and have enough confidence to step forward.

People who learn to trust themselves also practice having more trust in the future. The result is that they become more confident, more self-reliant, and more able to deal with whatever comes their way.

People who are willing to trust in the future also tend to take carefully calculated risks—that is, they are willing to have courage, overcome hesitation and fear, open their thinking to positive possibilities, and move forward.

People who learn trust create more successes in their lives. They do that because by learning to trust in themselves, they affect everything else about them.

*   *   *

*Why **trust** matters:*
The opposite of a mindset of trust is a mindset of doubt. Without trust, you cannot rely on yourself, on others, or on the future. *With* a mindset of trust, you extend the faith you have in yourself to the belief you have in others. You adopt a sense of confidence that encourages you to venture forward—instead of holding back out of insecurity or fear. Trust is an essential choice, without which you can never freely move forward, and never really live.

*   *   *

Using *trust* in a phrase of positive self-talk:

"Because I choose to trust myself, I am able to trust others, and I am able to trust in my future. The more I practice trusting myself, the better I get, and the brighter my future becomes."

27. Compassion

True compassion rises above—and stands apart from—status, wealth, power, image, or personal ego. Compassion is one of the deepest emotions a human can feel, and the truest form of compassion occurs when you feel genuine empathy and concern for others—without benefit to yourself.

Compassion often has a price. It requires your willingness to feel deeply and honestly for someone or something outside of yourself. And it requires that you care without expecting anything in return—other than a sense of knowing that your heart is good, and you're expressing it well.

Compassion is a form of bonding with others that makes you uniquely 'human.' *Without* compassion, you can become distant and disconnected, and never feel the hurt or the pain that someone else must endure. *With* compassion, you feel for others in a way that connects you to them and allows you to share your humanity with theirs, and their humanity with yours.

*   *   *

*Why **compassion** matters:*
There is no true happiness, and no
ultimate success as an individual, without
having a genuine sense of compassion for
others. True compassion rises from the soul;
it is the ultimate, binding human quality that
makes all of us *one.*

*   *   *

Using **compassion** in a phrase of positive
self-talk:

*"I have compassion. I am a person of
quality, and I care deeply about others. I
listen carefully for my compassion to speak to
me, and when it does, I am always ready to
understand, help, support, love, care, give,
and share."*

28. Charity

Charity—which I best define as *"caring* in the form of *giving"*—is one of the choices in life that is usually left up to the conscience of the individual. It is also a sometimes confusing word. This is because, in the same moment, charity can be an act of selflessness, an act of love, compassion, and thankfulness—or it can be an act of duty, penance, overcoming guilt, or piousness.

It is clear, however, that no one can be called truly successful at living without having within themselves a strong sense and expression of charity—caring for and helping others—however they choose to express that charity in their lives.

*   *   *

*Why **charity** matters:*
The opposite of a charity mindset is to think in a self-serving way. There are times that may be necessary, but as an overall approach to life, *giving* makes us happier than *receiving*. So, having a charity mindset creates a win-win—both for the person of

need, who is the receiver, and for the one who gives.

*   *   *

Using **charity** in a phrase of positive self-talk:

"I care about others, and it shows. In my life, I choose to make charity—caring about others, and helping them improve their lives––an important part of who I am, and why I am here."

29. Service

When you live in *service* to others, you unleash a positive, natural force in your life. When your goal is to help other people do better, and you act on that goal, you receive an intrinsic reward that gives meaning to your day, uplifts your spirit, and enriches your soul.

Living your life in service to others is different from occasionally helping someone in need. It is an underlying *direction* in your life. It gives you a moral compass that identifies your purpose, informs your choices, and keeps you focused on what you value most. Living in service to others is a beautiful way to live.

*   *   *

*Why **service** matters:*
The opposite of a service mindset is not necessarily a negative mindset; it is a lack of awareness, or a lack of choice to focus on serving others. But it is when you choose to have a service mindset that you receive the rewards of doing something that is helpful,

worthwhile, and fulfilling—and to many, essential.

*   *   *

Using *service* in a phrase of positive self-talk:

"I have made the choice to live my life in service to others. That means I help, support, build, encourage, and believe in other people in my life. I make sure I take care of myself and meet my needs, but I make sure I always consider what I can do for others."

30. Empathy

Empathy is a kindred spirit of *compassion* and of *caring*. It is, universally, one of the most important words any of us can know, and one of the most important human qualities we can feel or express. It is a great part of what makes us human. And yet, not everyone has, or feels, empathy in the same way.

Your empathy is the amount of compassionate understanding you have for others. But because of our individual genes, and because of the way our brains are wired, some people have more natural empathy, and some people have less.

Fortunately, you can increase the amount of empathy and caring you have for others by choosing to do so—by turning up the volume on your "Empathy Meter." You can choose to accentuate it. Empathy can be heightened by deep listening, sensing, and practicing being 'in the mind' and 'in the heart' of the other person, experiencing and feeling as they do.

Having a high level of empathy is important in anything you do that involves other people. No one lives a fully-realized, quality life without it. And when you emphasize your empathy, along with your support, the people around you often do better—which, because of your empathy, is something you care about.

*   *   *

*Why **empathy** matters:*
Without a sense of empathy, people fail to exercise understanding, caring, and compassion—all of which are necessary for relating to others. Practicing having a strong sense of empathy not only gives you important insight into the people around you, it increases your understanding and elevates your level of humanity.

*   *   *

Using *empathy* in a phrase of positive self-talk:

"I have empathy, understanding, caring, and compassion for others. I don't just have *empathy, I* practice *it. And because I care with intention, it shows in everything I do."*

31. Listen

No one should have to be reminded of the power and importance of the simple word *listen*—as a rule of living. And yet, it is the exceptional person who follows the rule and learns the real art of listening. Instead, many people often take this amazing skill entirely for granted. They hear but they do not listen; they listen but they do not hear.

To the success person, *listen* is an *action* word. People who live at their fullest have learned to listen differently, in two important ways: First, they have taught themselves to listen with conscious intention and attention, with *focus*. During a conversation, they actually hear what is being said—*everything* that is said. Second, success people listen with insight and with intuition, so they also hear the *meaning* of what is being said, and they hear what is *not* being said.

To test your own listening skills, the next time you have a conversation with someone, make it a point to focus *entirely* on the other person—not on your own thoughts, but on *their* thoughts, both spoken and unspoken.

Watch them, focus on them only, with an open and clear interest in what they're saying. And consciously be aware of not only every word they say, but also of what might be going on in their mind, and what they're trying to express.

That kind of mindfulness and focused attention lead to the highest level of quality in your dealings with others—from family members, to work associates, to total strangers. The way you *listen* will distinguish you, set you apart, give you more insight, and help you succeed.

* * *

*Why **listen** matters:*
Without active listening, you typically hear no more than the normal noise level of life around you. The value of focusing on learning to listen is to make listening a skill that you choose to master. When you do, you hear more, perceive more, learn more, and understand more. That's something success people practice.

* * *

Using *listen* in a phrase of positive self-talk:

"I am a super listener. I practice improving my listening skills every day, with everyone I talk with. Instead of thinking of what I'm going to say next, I have learned to listen, with deep understanding, to what the other person is saying to me."

32. Love

It makes no sense to limit the concept of *love* by trying to define it. Throughout time, the number of pages writers have devoted to the subject of love is infinite.

So, for our purposes here, I will only briefly present my perspective on how important love is to all of us, and how essential love itself is to all success people. It would not be going too far to say that, for many of them, *love is the energy that gives purpose to consciousness and, ultimately, guides the growth of the universe itself.*

In a very practical way, when you focus on how much love you share or give in your life, it could seem to some that your priority or your focus should, instead, be on your work or your income or on other responsibilities.

But love *should* be a priority. Without love, people are empty and unfulfilled. With enough love, people are complete, and find their value and their purpose. People who are the most successful as quality human beings are determined to have love in their lives—in many ways. They recognize that love is the greatest of all positive motivations. *Love* is the essence of *positive*. And positive is the essence of success.

*   *   *

*Why **love** matters:*
Ultimately, love may be all that really matters. Without love, and a loving sense of 'being,' the world, and life itself, can be a difficult, tragic, and unrewarding place in which to exist. *With* a sense of abiding love, the world changes, and becomes an acceptable, often times even beautiful, place to learn and grow, and fulfill our promise. Love changes everything.

*   *   *

Using *love* in a phrase of positive self-talk:

"I bring love into my life every day. Each day, from the first moments when I awake, I open my heart to the love that has been given to me, and I think about the ways, today, that I can share that love with others, and add to the love that I bring to the world."

Chapter 5

The Secret Words for
Wiring Your Brain for Success

The words we cover in this chapter will help you make sure you're doing everything you can do to wire your brain in the very best way.

This is where personal growth combines with neuroscience. Today, more and more success people understand that the reason for their success has to do with how their brain is programmed, and how they act on the programs they have that are strongest. The better your programs, the greater chance you have of making everything work.

This is why understanding the role of self-talk in your life is so important. When you listen to your own self-talk, you're hearing a playback of the programs you have recorded and stored in your brain. (On average, as much as 77% of our programs are negative, counter-productive, or work against us.) And every day, usually without your even being aware of those programs, your brain is automatically acting on the programs you have that are the strongest.

This is why success people, especially those who make it a point to be aware of their programs, practice a lot of positive self-talk:

a. The right self-talk wires positive programs into your brain.

b. Positive programs create a positive attitude.

c. A positive attitude results in making good choices.

d. Good choices result in taking the right actions.

e. The right actions create successful results.

As you can see, there is a direct link between your self-talk, your programs, and your success.

When you become aware of the programs you have now, and replace the programs that are working *against* you with positive, new programs that work *for* you, you vastly improve your chances for success.

As you read through the secret words in this chapter, you'll get an inside look at how the most progressive success people think about their own programs and what they do about them. These words give me a tremendous respect for the human brain— and what it will do to help us succeed. And fortunately, we have learned how to program our brains to do that.

We'll start with the word that is at the center of our success. It is the word *brain*.

33. Brain

The field of personal growth has long focused on the role of the human *mind* in creating individual success. But we're now changing our focus to studying what is behind the mind—the science of the brain itself.

In today's world of neuroscience, people who want to achieve the best in their lives recognize the key role the brain—and therefore, their mind—plays in everything they think and do.

Your brain, and how it becomes 'wired,' is the single most important player in your success. If your brain is wired to help you succeed, chances are you will. If your brain is wired to make you fail, failure is what you can expect.

The key is to be aware that, at all times, your words and your thoughts are actually wiring your brain to create your successes— or your failures. Take care of your brain. Give it the right input. Give it the right messages, the right words, and it will help you achieve anything that is possible.

* * *

*Why **brain** matters:*
Within ourselves, other than spirit, our brain is all we've got to guide us. Without being aware of what a well-managed brain can do for them, people fail more often than necessary, and they have little understanding of why things are going wrong. The more you understand and manage your brain, the more you will be able to successfully manage your mind—and your life.

* * *

Using **brain** in a phrase of positive self-talk:

"I make sure I always give the right messages to my brain. I know that every thought I think, and every word I say, will wire my brain for success or failure. So I always give my brain the right messages—the words that help me do my very best, in every area of my life."

34. Programs

The word *programs*, here, refers to the messages that get wired into our brains, and cause us to think and act the way we do. We've learned from the field of neuroscience that the messages we receive repeatedly—either from the world around us or from our own self-talk—are actually wired into the brain. And the brain acts on those wired-in programs as though they are true—whether they're true or not.

The key to programming is *repetition*. Everything you believe about yourself is the result of repeated messages that have been stored as programs in your brain. Everything you believe about your future, your capabilities, how smart you are, and even the likelihood of your success—or your failure—is based on those programs.

Taking advantage of the brain's neuroplasticity (the ability of the brain to rewire itself based on new input), success people practice self-talk that is healthy and practical, and that will also help them grow. People whose self-talk is realistic, but positive, create programs in their brains that help them succeed.

*   *   *

*Why **'programs'** matters:*
The person who is not aware of the *programs* they're receiving—or how programs work—leaves his or her programing up to chance. Being aware that you can rewire your brain with healthy new programs, and taking dedicated action to do so, puts you in control of your programing—which affects everything else about you.

*   *   *

Using **programs** in a phrase of positive self-talk:

"I know that my programs are the result of the messages I receive that are repeated most often. So I choose to give my brain the right self-talk messages. I make sure that my self-talk is positive, healthy, and always creates the programs that are best for me."

35. Repetition

I have touched on the importance of repetition in several areas of this book. That's because success people understand that *repetition is the secret to success*. It is repetition that creates our mental images of ourselves, and forms all of our attitudes and our beliefs. So, repetition is a powerful tool.

It is through the use of *repetition* that carefully-worded self-talk phrases—like the kind I've written for you in these pages—are wired into your brain. They are the healthy, positive kinds of programs your brain requires to help you live as a successful person.

It is *repetition* that creates all of your habits, tells you who you are, creates your picture of your future, and causes you to take the steps to live it out.

Control what is *repeated* to your brain, and you will take control of your life.

* * *

*Why **repetition** matters:*

The discovery of *repetition* as a key to rewiring the brain is one of the most important breakthroughs to emerge from the fields of neuroscience and personal growth. People who are aware of the power of repetition are able to increase the number of positive programs in their brain. By doing that they ensure that the programs they have that are the *strongest,* are also the most *helpful.*

* * *

Using **repetition** in a phrase of positive self-talk:

"I make sure I always use repetition to wire my brain with the strongest, healthiest, most positive self-talk. The more I hear it, the truer it becomes."

36. Learn

This is one of my favorite words. (Ok, they're *all* my favorites.) But the word 'learn' is special. That's because from birth on, *learning* is where everything starts—and the opportunity to learn is what creates our progression throughout our lives.

As infants, we were born with a brain that was designed to keep us safe, to regulate our internal controls—and to *learn*. There are almost no limitations on how much we can learn. We move from infant to child to youth to young adult to mature adult—and when we get there, our brain hasn't come close to learning what it is capable of learning.

Every time you learn something, you create new neural networks and connections in your brain. I love the idea of learning, because it is an endless opportunity to rewire, to grow; to change from nothing to something—from ordinary to extraordinary. That's why so many people who are excelling in their lives love learning; there is no end to how much they can learn and how much better they can become. To the success person, life isn't about getting by—it's about *growing*. And that's what *learning* is all about.

* * *

*Why **learn** matters:*
Learn is another of the secret words that is foundational to a mindset of personal growth. Philosophers have suggested that our primary purpose in life is to *learn*—and thereby to *grow*. Having a mindset that focuses on learning makes personal growth a natural and ongoing part of your progress as an individual.

* * *

Using ***learn*** in a phrase of positive self-talk:

"I love to learn, and I love to grow. Every day is a new opportunity for me to learn in so many ways. It's not just my years of school or my education that counts; my life and my future are up to me—and what I learn today, tomorrow, and every day."

37. Thoughts

Your *thoughts* are the driving force behind all of your goals and achievements. In fact, your thoughts literally wire your brain for success or failure. That's what self-talk is all about; it's your self-talk that controls the thoughts that create your success.

It is when you recognize the immense power of your *thoughts*—and what they are able to create—that you can begin to glimpse the amount of control you actually have over your own life.

Learning to manage your thoughts can sound like a big task. However, your brain is designed to change—to be rewired with new input. And anyone who chooses, can change their input. So the message is clear: When you change your thoughts, you rewire—and change—your brain. When you change your brain, what follows is, you change your life.

* * *

*Why **'thoughts'** matters:*

When you are not consciously selecting them, your thoughts are wiring your brain without your consent. When that happens, anything can happen—and it is often not for the best. When you are aware of all of your thoughts—when you consciously control and direct them—you are personally taking charge of the programming of your brain. That is one of the most important responsibilities—and greatest blessings—you will ever have.

*   *   *

Using ***thoughts*** in a phrase of positive self-talk:

"I understand the power of my thoughts. I am in control of me, so I manage every thought I think. I make sure I always have the thoughts that wire my brain with positive and with success—in every area of my life."

38. Positive

If the secret words in this book were presented in order of how valuable they are, one of the first words on the list would have to be the word *positive*. What an amazing, incredible, life-changing, powerful, and essential word *'positive'* is. All of the other success words are enhanced and strengthened by the positive mental environment in which you use them.

There is a reason for this. As I mentioned in Chapter 1, thinking in the *positive* wires more neural networks into the left, pre-frontal cortex of your brain—a part of the brain that helps you confront problems and find solutions, and puts you into action.

I'm not referring to any sort of 'Pollyanna positive'—wishful thinking without a practical, realistic foundation to base it on. Quite the opposite. The right, effective, positive thinking is far different from that. The form of positive we're referring to here is highly practical and grounded in no-nonsense reality.

The concept of *thinking in the positive* has moved from just being a popular word of choice for success people, to being a recognized product of brain functioning that is studied by neuroscientists and prescribed by psychologists. *Thinking in the positive literally rewires your brain to help you succeed.* No sincere person, who wants to create a successful life, can do without it.

* * *

*Why **positive** matters:*
The opposite of a positive mindset is to see the world as a dark, negative place, with minimal opportunity to excel, and little chance for joy. A negative mindset fosters a belief that life is made up of endless struggles and pointless challenges—with no end of negative in sight. Having a *positive mindset* reveals the reality of vast, unlimited promise and potential, while it opens your eyes to the endless opportunities and the joy of living that await you. All of that *good* is the natural result of having a mindset that is *positive*.

* * *

Using *positive* in a phrase of positive self-talk:

"I think positive! I, alone, control my thoughts, and I choose to add to my brain those thoughts that are helpful, healthy, and beneficial. Throughout my life and throughout my day, I think positive."

39. Perspective

Your *perspective* literally controls how you look at life. And how you look at life controls how you think and the actions you take. So, your perspective directly affects what you do, and how successful you will be at anything.

Your perspective is the view from which you see your life—and anything in it. It's a brain thing. All of your perspectives are shaped by the programs you have stored in your subconscious mind. Your beliefs and your views on anything are based on the programs you received from others, or from your own self-talk.

Those programs that become wired into your brain are not based on *truth*—they are based on *repetition*. And how often the programs are repeated determines how strongly they become wired into your brain.

This is why the negative person has a negative perspective and looks at the world in a negative way. It's also why the positive person sees the world in a completely different way—from a positive perspective.

Same opportunity, two different people, two different sets of programs and two entirely different outcomes.

Your perspective can be *uncertain, negative, suspicious, hopeless,* and *doomed for failure.* Or, your perspective can be *bright, positive, capable, enthusiastic, hopeful, promising,* and *successful.* Choose the path you want to take, and support your choice with the self-talk that will help you get there.

* * *

Why **perspective** *matters:*
The person with a diminished perspective sees the world through a narrow lens. It is a limited view that never shows the true picture or the infinite scope of possibility that exists—they're just not able to see it. Having a *broad perspective* mindset brings together vision, clarity, knowledge, and truth—and gives you a more accurate picture of the world around you.

* * *

Using **perspective** in a phrase of positive self-talk:

"I have a great perspective on life. I see life, every day, from the higher position of positive, 'can-do' possibility. That's a perspective I live up to in everything I think, and everything I do."

40. Focus

The word *focus* is another *action* word, and it is a good word to learn to love. It is one of the essential words in the vocabulary of success. Focus is the action of turning all of your energy and attention toward one thing——and one thing only. (Focus is the opposite of multi-tasking.) It is a person's highly-focused energy and attention that sets ideas on fire.

A perfect metaphor for focus is that of a magnifying glass. When you are sitting on a lawn of grass on a clear summer day, hold a magnifying glass (of only two or three inches in diameter) a few inches above the cool grass beneath it. The sun's rays, when focused, will create a small, brightly-lighted spot on the grass.

Within moments, that point of light will begin to smoke, and then, with the intensity of the rays focused on it, the grass will burst into flame. From what seems like *nothing*, you have created intense heat and fire. All of that, on a cool day, with less sunlight than reaches the flowers on your kitchen windowsill.

When you actively focus your attention and energy on one specific task or idea, you are 'gathering' energy, drawing that energy in, like a magnifying glass, and directing it to the goal you're focusing on. To get good at creating super-focus, you may have to practice doing it—until the high-energy intensity of positive focus becomes natural and easy for you—but it is well worth it. Purposely creating focus is something that all of the success people do.

*   *   *

*Why **focus** matters:*
A mindset of *focus* is an indispensable tool. Without focus, you can wander through each day without ever feeling like you've accomplished anything of value. And the greatest opportunities in front of you fall to the wayside from a lack of dedicated attention. *With* a mindset of focus, you give yourself clarity, you identify your priorities, you seize the opportunity and the day, and you create the mental energy required to get the job done.

*   *   *

Using *focus* in a phrase of positive self-talk:

"I practice having incredible focus. I am able to focus my energy and my attention on one single idea or task at a time. And because I do, I am more successful than ever."

41. Clarity

Clarity means seeing past your own prejudices and your own preconceptions about anything. Doing that can be difficult. However, having clarity—seeing *truth*—is vitally important.

The problem is that having true clarity about anything is difficult, because we see everything through the lens of our own mental programs—which, along the way, got wired into our brains. But just because something got wired in, doesn't mean it's true. In fact, a lot of what gets wired into each of our brains *isn't* true.

As much as you can, question everything and seek the truth. Instead of thinking you already have the answer, force yourself to be willing to be open to ideas and opinions that may be different from your own.

Always keep in mind that what you believe to be true is actually a set of programs that your brain has wired in and is now acting on as though those programs are true—whether they are true or not.

* * *

*Why **clarity** matters:*

A mindset that lacks clarity cannot see what is right and what isn't. Without clarity, there is no certainty; your perceptions are easily distorted by mental programs that may be completely false. *With* clarity, your perceptions are more accurate—and truth stands out. When you have a mindset of clarity, you practice searching for what is *real*—and you're able to see more of the world as it really is.

* * *

Using **clarity** in a phrase of positive self-talk:

"Because I choose to see the world in the clearest possible way, I look for the clarity of truth in everything I see."

42. Vision

People with *vision* see beyond what other people see. Having vision is about being able to see past the day, beyond the average, sending your imagination into the future, or seeing something beyond the ordinary and gaining a perspective of greater depth and insight.

The kind of vision we're talking about here is the amazing ability you have to expand your thinking beyond your day-to-day experience—seeing what you cannot otherwise see. Having vision is a skill, one you can practice and improve, that allows you to see things in a different way, and recognize the awakening of something new— or newly revealed—in the process.

When you practice having vision, you look beyond the moment, perceive what may lie ahead—or what your imagination is showing you—and expand your *thinking* to meet the *possibility*.

*   *   *

*Why **vision** matters:*

Vision, as we're using it here, is *'seeing in your mind.'* Living *without* vision is like being sedated while living in a mental box in the dark with blinders on. Practicing having vision takes you out of the box. And the more vision you have, the more clearly, the better, and the farther you can see.

* * *

Using **vision** in a phrase of positive self-talk:

"I have vision. I practice seeing beyond the day and beyond the ordinary. Because I have vision, I am able to expand my thinking, discover more positive possibilities, and make them a part of my life."

Chapter 6

The Secret Words for
Creating the Very Best You

The secret words in this chapter are all about you, and who you see yourself to be.

With what we know about the brain and programming, as we saw in the previous chapter, it would only make sense to make sure the programs that make you who you *are*, are the best programs you can get.

If you ask yourself whether you have any programs that cause you problems, or could be holding you back, what would you say? Or if you could choose any programs that would make you a better, stronger, more successful, secure person, what would they be?

In this chapter, we look at the secret words success people use to identify how they feel about themselves—the programs that give them their identity and shape how they look at life each day. See how much of yourself you find in these words. Keep in mind that if you'd like to have more of these qualities in your life, you can.

The first of these qualities is a word that is often misunderstood. It is *self-esteem*.

NOTE: To download the free user tools—*The Secret Words Workbook, The Secret Words Poster, Six Weeks to Success* home coaching program, and *Personal Goal-Setting Forms*—see Chapter 12, or go to:
www.thesecretwordsofsuccess.com/tools

---

43. Self-Esteem

Self-esteem is a term that is often interpreted, incorrectly, to just mean 'self-love.' But it's different from that; it's more than that.

In my clarification, your self-esteem is not necessarily how much you *love* yourself—it is how you *see* yourself. Your self-esteem is your self-*estimation* of yourself—your personal picture of who you believe yourself to be.

Your self-esteem includes anything that you believe about yourself: how smart you are, what you're good at, what you're *not* good at, how you deal with others, how you look, what dreams you have, what you plan to do with your future, and the chances of your making that future happen.

All of that is part of your *self-esteem,* which means your complete, comprehensive picture of who you believe yourself to be.

Your self-esteem is one of the most important measures of who you are. The picture of you that you hold in your mind is the template upon which all of the opportunities in your life will be drawn. How you see yourself controls how your brain responds to every opportunity—good, bad, promising, or life-changing—that comes your way.

So, your *self-esteem* is not just about how much you like yourself or love yourself. It is about how much you *believe* in yourself. It's about how much you believe in *you* being able to step forward, and always find the best in yourself—and the amazing opportunities that are in front of you.

*   *   *

Why **self-esteem** *matters:*
A quality picture of yourself in your mind (positive self-esteem) creates a quality *you*. Your attitude about yourself determines how you treat yourself, how you educate yourself, how you train yourself to be, how you deal with others, how you think, how you express yourself, how you see yourself and your future, and how well you do in life. It all begins with your self-esteem.

*   *   *

Using **self-esteem** in a phrase of positive self-talk:

"I have strong, healthy self-esteem. I like the real me. And the real me is strong, positive, and capable. I believe in myself, and every day, I have strong, positive self-esteem, and I'm glad to be me."

44. Value

A key to becoming the person you were intended to be, is the extent to which you recognize your own *value*—your own worth as an individual. Your value is not just about your self-esteem; it is a measure of your complete, limitless, intrinsic worth. And you are more valuable than you can possibly know.

People who find value only in external possessions—things of temporary material worth—often end up unhappy, or at a minimum, they miss what life is really about. They don't see that the real value is in themselves, rather than in the things they own. As a result, their focus in life is on what they have *around* them, rather than what they have *within* them.

In your own life, the greatest thing of value you have is *you*—and what you do with your life. It might be fine to have riches and possessions, but the greatest riches you will ever have are those you possess within yourself. And as the self-talk below points out, one way your value is reflected is in how

much value—true goodness—you add to the
lives of others.

* * *

*Why **value** matters:*
Your personal value is your self-worth—
which is something only you can determine.
So, *you* are the appraiser of your value. Your
appraisal is important, because the value you
place on yourself will determine most of the
choices you make in a day or in a lifetime—
the friends you choose, how you allow people
to treat you, the kind of work you do, the
kinds of challenges you accept, and every
other part of your life. Your personal *value*
sets your standards.

* * *

Using **value** in a phrase of positive self-
talk:

*"I have value in my life. I value myself,
and I value the people I care about. A true
reflection of my own worth is the value I add
to the lives of others."*

45. Dignity

Having *dignity* is an art, a skill, an attitude, a belief in yourself, and a way of life. In public, dignity is when you rise above the moment, hold your head high, exercise grace, and call upon your highest qualities to be evident as you play out the scene. In private, dignity is when you do the same.

You can choose to do anything you do, with dignity. It is a state of mind that presents a picture of the highest quality of your character. And if you practice it, true dignity is with you always. It was once thought that only rulers, or kings and queens or people of high stature, had dignity. But now, at a time when you're able to rule yourself and your own life in almost every way, you get to have it, too.

Try it for yourself. Right now, take a deep breath, lift your chin slightly, square your shoulders, and in spite of any misgivings you may have about yourself, look out at the world in front of you with a sense of *wisdom*, *confidence*, and *quiet strength*. That's a touch of what dignity feels like.

Living with a sense of *dignity* is a wonderfully uplifting, positive, self-esteem-building way to live. It tells the world around you that you are a person of quality and character. And it says the same thing to you.

*   *   *

*Why **dignity** matters:*
The opposite mindset to that of having dignity causes you to show the world a lesser expression of yourself. No one experiences lasting well-being without living with a sense of dignity. Having a mindset that places a high value on dignity is the surest way to ensure that people around you will respect you. That's because having dignity shows that you have a high degree of respect for *yourself.*

*   *   *

Using *dignity* in a phrase of positive self-talk:

"I have dignity. I practice having dignity every day. I am a person of quality and character. And because I choose to live up to my best, I practice having dignity, no matter what the situation may be. Every day of my life, I have dignity."

46. Manners

Manners is an action word. It requires that you present yourself in a way that shows you at your best, while also showing respect for the people around you.

It is unfortunate that more children aren't taught manners today the way they were in the past. It's unfortunate because, if more adults practiced having manners today, we would all live in a more civilized world.

But people who are living a quality, successful life, have figured that out. For people who are making life work, having manners is as important today as it ever was.

Your manners are a signal to others. And what your manners signal is consciously (and unconsciously) highly revealing. People with manners have *deference* for others. They are exceptionally *courteous*. They *respect* others, and they show it. They are *polite*. They show you by their words and by their actions that, no matter who you are, they care about you, that you're important—that you *count*.

People with manners do the obvious—like holding the door for others to pass through. But they do more than that: they still say *please* and *thank you* and *excuse me*, and they mean it. They share, willingly. They respect other people's possessions. They wait for their own turn to speak. They respect other people's opinions. And they treat others with understanding, openness, and honesty.

When you're talking to a person with manners, they don't just *kind of* listen to you, they *listen*—and they listen without interrupting. They are focused entirely on you. They look you in the eye. They ask questions that show a genuine interest in you. They respect you for who you are, and not because of your title or your job description; they respect you for who you are as a human being.

That's just a brief sample of what mannered people do. To the success person, having manners is not just an occasional thing; *it's a way of life*. Having manners is one of the reasons they're successful. And they practice having *manners* every single day.

*   *   *

Why **'manners'** *matters:*
A lack of quality manners signals a disdain and a lack of respect—both for yourself and for others. Exhibiting poor manners brands you as having limited empathy—and either a lack of training or a low level of self-worth. When you practice having a *high level* of manners—in all situations—you immediately stand out as an exceptional person. Having *good* manners opens the door to acceptance, approval, admiration, and respect from others.

*   *   *

Using **manners** in a phrase of positive self-talk:

"I practice having manners, at all times and in all situations. I am a quality person, and it shows. I practice caring, listening, showing respect, showing humility, being thoughtful, always being courteous, and so much more. I am a picture of quality and character. I have manners."

47. Virtue

Virtue was taught by Plato as being *"the highest form of moral thought and conduct."* As we're using it here, virtue means *living up to the highest possible level of your being, in every area of your life.*

Many years ago, the concept of *virtue* was taught to every school-aged child as an important instruction in how to live a character-centered life.

In just six simple letters, that one small word—*virtue*—means: *honesty, trust, moral quality, worthiness, integrity, judgement, strength of character,* and *humility.* All of that in one word!

While the concept of virtue may not be taught in the same way to school children today, if you have kids, of any age, you may want to teach them the word *'virtue,'* and tell them what it really means.

As a success person, you will also want to add this amazing word to your personal list of words to think about often, and use as a standard by which you deal with anything. Living a life of virtue, works. No one can be perfect, but practicing *virtue*—to the highest level you can—is essential to living a life of lasting personal success.

*   *   *

*Why **virtue** matters:*
The opposite of a virtue mindset is one of lowered expectations of yourself, with less effort put into getting things right. Having a mindset of virtue says that you want to live up to a high standard in all things, and you choose to live at your maximum potential as a person of quality. That's something that can be difficult to do, but it is a worthy quest. And you will always do better because of it.

*   *   *

Using *virtue* in a phrase of positive self-talk:

"I am a person of quality and character. I know the value of always living up to my best. And I live up to my best when I make virtue, in every way, an essential part of how I live my life."

48. Good

Good is the epitome of old-fashioned virtue. In the last century, *do* good, *think* good, *be* good were the admonitions good parents passed on to their children—teaching them to live what would become honorable lives.

That was a time when foundational values were taught and understood by most people. *Good* isn't a new or passing idea. Ancient philosophers taught that *'good'* was the superlative—*the highest level of being.*

When it is your personal goal to live up to your best, basing your choices on the concept of *good,* gives you a reliable guide to follow. The decision to *'go for the good'* assures you that whatever the outcomes of your actions, they will always be based on the most positive intent.

* * *

Why **good** *matters:*
The choice to *'be a good person in order to live a good life'* may be a simple choice, but it

is also profound. If the notion of *good* does not often cross your mind, it is possible to ignore it, and become oblivious to the consequences of living without it. Keeping in mind that the historical opposite of good is 'evil,' it makes sense to have a mindset that is clearly *good*. If it isn't good, no good can come of it.

*   *   *

Using **good** in a phrase of positive self-talk:

"I choose to always follow the path of good. I know that the highest levels of knowledge and truth stem from the quest for good—and the quest for good is an important part of my life."

49. Honesty

We all know that honesty is an important trait to have in our relationships with others. But it is also an essential trait to have in your relationship with yourself. When you look into a mirror, directly into your eyes, and ask yourself the questions, *"How am I doing? What do I need to work on most? Am I winning or losing? Am I living up to my promise?"*—what kinds of answers do you get?

The reason honesty is so important to people who choose to be successful is that honesty is the internal regulator that tells them if they are on track. For you to be successful, and stay that way, your internal compass has to be accurate; it has to be *honest.*

People who are successful within themselves practice being honest with others—and just as clear and honest with their own inner selves. Doing that isn't always easy. But, with faithful practice, honesty becomes a habit—a conditioned part of your character. If you look for it, you can see it in your eyes.

Think about that the next time you look into a mirror.

* * *

*Why **honesty** matters:*
The opposite of an honesty mindset is self-delusion and the avoidance of reality. When you choose an honesty mindset, and live by it, you have a chance of seeing what really is. So you have more clarity, more integrity, and you reward yourself with greater understanding. That allows you to deal with life as it is, not just how you'd like it to be.

* * *

Using **honesty** in a phrase of positive self-talk:

"I choose to be honest—with others, and with myself. Being honest lets me see the details of my life in a clear and accurate way. Because I'm honest, I know who I am and where I'm going. And because I'm honest, the path I choose is always clear."

50. Humility

Humility happens when you lower your own stature or presence below what it may actually be—usually for the sake of someone else, or something you believe is greater than you. That means no matter how highly you might think of yourself, you still have the ability to show true deference for something greater.

Humility, the opposite of vanity, also means that you never get too big in your own mind. If you were a mountain, unless you were Mount Everest, there would always be other mountains that would be higher than you. Success people know they are fortunate to be where they are, and they are confident enough to show respect and deference for others around them.

Humility, in its ultimate grace, is being able to lower your head below someone else's, simply because, in spite of your strengths, you are able to honor and respect the qualities of others—and you understand your reason for being here in the first place.

*   *   *

*Why **humility** matters:*
It is the person of greatness who kneels with dignity. *Without* humility we are less our true selves and more a pretense, a facade we use to hide our failings. *With* humility we take off the mask and allow the world to see us as we actually are—standing tall, courageous perhaps, but just trying to do our best. It is our *humility* that lets us find our true stature; it is the person with the bowed head who stands the tallest.

*   *   *

Using ***humility*** in a phrase of positive self-talk:

"Humility and respect are strong in my life. I am grateful for all that I am, and all that I have, and I make sure that vanity never plays a role in any part of my life."

51. Spirit

Spirit is an unusual secret word. Nothing about it is concrete or touchable; and yet, having a high level of spirit can be experienced, and even practiced. Success people practice lifting their spirit at any time—or perhaps they are having their *spirit* uplift *them.*

The word 'spirit' has many meanings. For the success person, one of the most practiced uses of the word 'spirit' is aligned with an attitude or an emotion that is uplifting or energizing in a way that seems to go beyond the purely physical—as though you are calling on a higher state of mind. It is an intangible concept, but it has tangible results.

This elevated sense of spirit is something almost everyone experiences from time to time. But it is something success people often practice having. They experience this heightened sense of spirit more than other people, because they are consciously aware of it, and because they call upon it, and create it at will.

149

When you're facing problems or challenges, this extra-energy mental uplift of spirit is abundantly helpful, because it immediately gives you more emotional strength; it lets you know you are capable, and can rise above the problem—with a higher, more positive sense of mental well-being—no matter what the circumstances.

To find out if you have a strong sense of this kind of spirit, you can test it for yourself. Sit silently for a few moments, and quiet your mind. Then, once quieted, ask yourself the question, *"How is my spirit?"* Your feeling, in that moment, will tell you what you need to know.

*   *   *

*Why **spirit** matters:*
The *opposite* of having a mindset of *spirit* is to be without the 'life force' needed to rise above life's problems. Without *spirit,* we lack the energy and the will to continue—to meet the challenges and overcome the setbacks. When you have a strong mindset of empowering spirit, you are imbued with a vitality that enlivens you mentally and

physically. The choice to *have* that spirit—
and make a *habit* of having it—is up to you.

* * *

Using **spirit** in a phrase of positive self-talk:

"I have spirit. I have strength, enthusiasm, and an unbelievably winning attitude about anything that is a part of my life. I have spirit, and I live my spirit every day of my life."

52. Competence

What will account *most* for your success? It's not just intelligence. It's not your degree. It's not luck. It's not your family and it's not status. It is something else that will determine how successful you will be— especially in your job or career: the number one determinant of your being successful is your *competence*—how *well* you do what you do. (In fact, the word *competence* includes, and derives from, the word *compete.)*

This doesn't mean that factors like your education, your experience, your drive, etc., don't make a difference; they do. They all play a part. But when you think about where you hope to go, or what you want to achieve, instead of relying on the list of attributes and credentials you would write on a resume', ask yourself the question *"How competent am I?"*

If you put in the effort it takes to become highly competent—*get really good at*— whatever it is you choose to do, you give yourself the highest chance of being successful. If you would like to achieve that, this is a word you should check or underline and re-read frequently.

* * *

*Why **competence** matters:*
In the outside world, a high level of competence is your most important asset. If you want to excel in the workplace, if that is important to you, the goal to create competency should be one of your primary goals. The investment you make in yourself is in time and effort—honing your skills, endlessly, to become one of the best. However, it is ultimately that investment that creates the difference between the 'haves' and the 'have nots.'

* * *

Using **competence** in a phrase of positive self-talk:

"I create competence. I know what I want to get good at—and I do everything I need to do, for as long as it takes, to become as good as I choose to be."

53. Maturity

For many people today, maturity means nothing more than reaching a certain age in life. But if you dig deeper, you begin to see that it isn't the physical age you've reached that counts—it's how much progress you've made within your *self*. It is how much you have grown.

At one time, maturity was measured by how wise a person had become—how much wisdom they had mastered. Today, for most people, maturity is measured by physical maturity, and less so by how mature you are mentally, emotionally, and spiritually.

Success people understand this. They set a goal to accumulate experience with meaning, to become as smart—with wisdom—as they can get. To the success people, the word 'mature' means *smart, experienced, understanding, together, wise,* and *able to handle things well*. And it has little to do with how old they are.

*   *   *

*Why **maturity** matters:*

The predictable thing about an adult mindset that does *not* possess maturity, is unnecessary hardship, trauma, and failure. A mindset that is not mature doesn't understand the 'reason' it lacks. Having a mindset of maturity keeps you mindful of thinking and acting in a measured, intelligent, reliable way. The outcome of which, is measured, intelligent, reliable results.

* * *

Using **maturity** in a phrase of positive self-talk:

"I choose to become the most mature, complete, together person I can become. I know that it's not my age that counts; it is the wisdom I gain, and my willingness to see my own life—in anything I do—in the most enlightened, practical, positive, and mature way."

54. Wisdom

Having *wisdom* is of such great value that people who have it always strive to have more of it. Wisdom is made up of a combination of *knowledge, experience, insight, reflection, under-standing,* and *foresight.* It is a magical shaping of one's mind that almost never comes with youth—and only occasionally comes with age.

Having wisdom carries with it many blessings—one of which is that of *not* doing or saying something you should not do or say. Wisdom is sometimes better at telling you what *not* to do next than telling you exactly what you *should* do next.

Perhaps wisdom's greatest quality, however, is that it gives you a preternatural sense of clarity about life in general. It instills in its bearer a *'knowing,'* an understanding of how life works—at many levels—and how to work within that life. Wisdom offers a broadly encompassing overview of the world—a perspective that allows you to deal with the present, and work to shape the future, while at the same time, learning to be at peace with the inevitable.

What is remarkable about wisdom is that if you want to have it, or have more of it, you can work to attain it. It takes a somewhat special person to do that, because it requires gathering the six attributes I mentioned above—*knowledge, experience, insight, reflection, understanding,* and *foresight.*

But, since you're reading this book, I would assume those are exactly the kinds of things you are interested in already.

* * *

Why **wisdom** *matters:*
Having wisdom lets you in on the secrets of life. A mindset of *wisdom* combines your knowledge and experience with insight and an open mind—giving you a more accurate, practical view of how life really works. The end result of wisdom is the exercise of good judgement. Without making wisdom a conscious quest, you can too easily forget its importance, and allow your mind to drift in a state of unexamined biases and inaccurate

beliefs. *With* wisdom, you not only think for yourself, you also view each moment from a higher, more objective, place—and elevate your thinking, and your choices, to a level that is above average.

* * *

Using **wisdom** in a phrase of positive self-talk:

"I seek to have true wisdom in my life. I make sure I am aware, at all times, of improving my knowledge, my experience, my insight, my reflection, my understanding, and my foresight. I am a student of wisdom, and I choose to have wisdom in my life."

Chapter 7

The Secret Words for
Creating a Success Attitude

When you meet someone who is living a quality life, you'll notice they have an attitude that is usually 'up'—positive, and healthy.

I know people like that, people whose attitude is almost never down, no matter what's happening in their life. They have an extra reserve of uplifting spirit—even during difficult times. And if they ever do get down, even for a moment, they come back fast, and stronger than ever.

Why is that? What is the special quality that keeps them strong, while living through the often difficult experiences of everyday living?

As we'll see from the words in this chapter, success people see a different picture of themselves, and a different picture of the world than others see—and it's a world that works. Imagine waking up every morning knowing you have created a foundation of the following words and traits in your own mind.

55. Character

The first secret word on the list for creating the foundation for a success attitude is *character*. The kind of character we're focusing on here is made up of a combination of traits that make us better beings in every way. Among them are *quality, honesty, virtue, humility, balance, understanding, trust, caring, resolution, determination,* and *endurance*. That is a remarkable assembly of attributes.

Character can be identified by observing whether, when confronted by a challenge of any kind, someone habitually takes the 'easy' way out—or whether they take the 'right' way out. In that situation, character is identified by the choices each person makes.

It's good to know that anyone who wants to have character—or more of it—can have it. However, to have it, you have to want to have it, and you have to work at it. The process of building character starts with practicing the attributes listed above—and wiring positive programs of those attributes into your brain.

Fortunately, those same attributes are also on the list of the secret words we're exploring in this book. So, if you'd like to make sure your character is the best, you're in the right place.

* * *

*Why **character** matters:*
Character is built one choice at a time. A mindset devoid of good character can only lead to a *downward* road of misguided steps, a life of conflict, and a lack of self-esteem. Instead of always having to struggle with the constant pitfalls a lesser character creates, a mindset of quality character allows you to focus on the opportunities and the possibilities of life—rather than being burdened with an excess of problems. If good character is your starting point, your road will still have its challenges, but it will always lead you upward.

* * *

Using *character* in a phrase of positive self-talk:

"I make good choices. I choose to have character of the highest level, in what I think, what I do, and how I live my life. I am a person of quality, and my choices—and my character—shows it."

56. Imagination

Imagination may be humankind's greatest earthly asset. Imagination is the place in our minds where all creativity begins. It is the birthplace of new ideas.

You were born with imagination, and it is a profoundly important gift. Today, your imagination is limited only by your mental programming, your desire to have an *active* imagination, and your determination to use it. The more you stretch the limits of your imagination, the more imagination you will have.

Imagination comes to us naturally as children, but most of what we have of it is taught *out* of us before we become adults. Fortunately, adults can regain their imagination by practicing opening their minds once again, and actively thinking beyond themselves—beyond their normal, everyday thinking.

Success people often appear to have more imagination than other people—and that's because they use their imagination more.

When successful people deal with opportunities or with problems, they are not afraid to rely on *imagination* to take them to the new vistas they seek or to help them find the answers they're looking for.

*   *   *

*Why **imagination** matters:*
A mind without imagination is like a lake without water. It is a dry, unimaginative place, a hollow, empty version of its once vibrant, living self. Within the human mind, imagination is the gateway—the essential *wellspring*; it is the source of *creativity, ideas, solutions, alternative solutions, opportunities, wonderful insights, and endless possibilities.* One of the greatest gifts you could ever receive is the gift of imagination. The wonderful thing is that with practice and insistence, imagination is a gift you can give to yourself.

*   *   *

Using *imagination* in a phrase of positive self-talk:

"I have imagination! I am always ready to think in new and different ways. I see the world, and everything in it, as filled with endless new opportunities, new ways to see things, and new ways to grow."

57. Attitude

Attitude is an action word—what you choose for your attitude is up to you and the internal action you take to change it. Attitude is a very important word on the list of success words, and a highly important word to all success people. Here's why:

Your attitude is the perspective from which you view life—and how you see anything within it. Almost everything you ever do will be driven by your attitude. That's why having an exceptional attitude—as opposed to a mediocre attitude or a bad attitude—is so important.

It is your attitude that allows you to see something as positive and doable—instead of something that is negative and impossible. It is your attitude that shows you a world that is filled with purpose, meaning, and endless opportunities, instead of seeing a world that is filled with limitations, misery and hardship.

What success people recognize is that attitude is a *choice*. Each individual's choice.

Always. Your attitude is never up to the world around you; your attitude is always up to you.

Instead of letting the day choose your attitude for you, you have within you the power to choose it for yourself. The attitude you choose each day will determine how well each day works for you. The attitude you have, overall, will determine how well your life works, overall.

* * *

*Why **attitude** matters:*
Changing your attitude is the one thing you can do, at any time, to change your reality—from one of seeing only difficulties and defeats, to one of counting your blessings and creating solutions. If there were one switch you carried with you that you could flip at any time to change your mental state, the label on that switch would read: *"Attitude."* Deciding to have a better attitude isn't self-delusion or wishful thinking. When you change your attitude, you modify the software in your brain that gives you your

168

picture of the world, operates your day, and controls your life.

*   *   *

Using *attitude* in a phrase of positive self-talk:

"I have a great attitude! I keep my attitude up, strong, healthy, and positive. I choose to see each day in the most positive, practical, healthy way. And because I do, I always have a great attitude!"

58. Energy

When related to your personal success, having energy means both having physical stamina and also being mentally alive and alert. A rule to remember is, *"The higher the interest, and the greater the focus, the more energy you create."*

Along with the normal, healthy lifestyle practice of keeping fit, add the practice of creating a high level of interest, super attention, and laser-sharp focus on anything you want to excel at doing. (In this case, no multi-tasking is allowed.) When you do this, your mental energy and your physical stamina will increase and help you operate at your best.

Anytime you hear yourself saying you don't have the energy you'd like to have, immediately change your self-talk to give yourself the kinds of messages that will create more energy, instead of insisting that you don't have enough.

*   *   *

*Why **energy** matters:*

People who have energy and focus accomplish more than people who are disinterested or distracted. Mental energy is created by interest. The more you become intensely involved in something—a project, a goal, or an idea, and the more you study it, explore it, and focus on it, the more mental *energy* you create, and the greater chance you have of turning it into something of value.

* * *

Using **energy** in a phrase of positive self-talk:

"I have energy! Because I am interested and focused, I not only have energy, I create more of it. And the more energy I have, the more interested and focused I become."

59. Enthusiasm

The word *'enthusiasm'* literally means *'God within.'* To have enthusiasm is to be filled with spirit—a strength that seems to come to you from something outside of you, or that is greater than you.

'Enthusiasm' and *'inspiration'* often go hand in hand, which is why people who frequently show enthusiasm are also often those who are able to create extraordinary things, or find unique and inspired solutions to problems.

The difficulty with enthusiasm is that it can be a challenge to get it if you don't have it. My own solution to this problem is to focus active attention on the idea or subject that I want to be enthusiastic about.

The more time you spend walking around your subject and studying it, the more you get to know it. The more curiosity and attention and interest you invest in the subject, the more the idea begins to blossom, and take on a life of its own. And when you see its potential begin to come to life, you will almost always find that it brings a natural sense of *enthusiasm* along with it.

*   *   *

*Why **enthusiasm** matters:*

In a child, it's called *excitement*. In an adult, it's called *enthusiasm*. But they are one and the same. In its most typical form, enthusiasm is seen when delight and energy burst to the surface, and your entire being is filled with a natural, joyful high. Although it is difficult to call up enthusiasm on demand, there are ways to create it. The best way is to have a high level of interest in something you enjoy. Active interest, plus enjoyment, creates enthusiasm.

*   *   *

Using *enthusiasm* in a phrase of positive self-talk:

"I choose to bring the powerful energy of enthusiasm to every worthwhile endeavor I pursue. When I want to create or accomplish something of importance to me, I make sure it has my attention, my interest, my action, and my enthusiasm."

60. Confidence

True *confidence* is earned through practice—and gaining experience. When the confidence-building person tries something new, they stay with it, and they practice doing it until they get it right. When they do, the successful experience brings confidence along with it. This 'duplicated experience' wires neural patterns into the brain which become more strongly imprinted through repetition.

Children are taught confidence by learning to do something often enough to get it right. Adults learn confidence the same way. Athletes, musicians, parents, teachers, business people, all get better with practice and experience. Add to that a 'can do' spirit, strong determination, and a desire to perform at your best, and you have the formula for *confidence*—and an important step toward success.

* * *

*Why **confidence** matters:*

Confidence is an asset that derives from experience. It can be pretended, but bluster never stands up to the real thing. A sense of self that lacks confidence will be hesitant to take necessary risks, and will fail to stand strong against opposition. A mindset that is *high* in confidence (without being over-confident) ensures that, when necessary, you will take the risk, you will be strong, you will endure, and you will have a good chance of winning.

* * *

Using ***confidence*** in a phrase of positive self-talk:

"I have confidence. I practice and repeat anything I want to master. And by doing that often—as often as it takes—I build confidence."

61. Determination

When you set a goal of any kind, how determined are you to reach it? Determination may not guarantee your success in achieving your goal, but your potential success is almost always directly proportionate to the amount of determination you bring to the task. When you ask yourself the question, *"How determined am I?"* the answer you give will usually predict the outcome.

We have all seen examples of someone who may have appeared to be less qualified than someone else to win an athletic event, but ended up winning because of his or her sheer determination to do so. The mythos of the underdog overcoming all odds and winning is an example of this; with determination, the seemingly impossible becomes possible.

Whatever weaknesses you have, determination makes them smaller. Whatever strengths you have, determination makes them greater.

*   *   *

*Why **determination** matters:*
There may be no greater force of will than *determination*. By itself, determination will help you defeat almost any challenge that is possible to overcome. What is remarkable about this great force is that it is entirely the result of the mindset you choose. While it can be bolstered by courage, determination itself requires only that you *choose* to have it, and refuse to accept anything less. Determination is your self-declared, inviolate line in the sand.

*   *   *

Using **determination** in a phrase of positive self-talk:

"Anytime I want to achieve something that is important to me, I make sure my goal is clear and my determination is strong. I always remember that the stronger my determination, the greater the chance of my success."

62. Endurance

Endurance is the ultimate defense against failure. It is also one of the greatest creators of success. If you have a dream that is possible and real—no matter what it is—and refuse to let it go, no matter what, there is a good chance you will succeed.

People often don't think about the importance of *endurance*, because today almost everyone lives in a push-button, channel-changing world in which little real endurance is required.

An old adage is that "survivors survive." The reason they do is almost always because they have *chosen* to survive—no matter what. The essence of survival—and ultimate success, is *endurance.*

* * *

*Why **endurance** matters:*
Born of determination, having a mindset of *endurance* gives you the advantage of winning the battle—by outlasting the problem. For those who recognize its great

179

value, *endurance* is a *life strategy*. The single notion of 'never giving up' is a powerful mantra for overcoming obstacles and achieving goals—and it is surpassed by little else. In the pursuit of achievement or victory, *endurance* prevails.

* * *

Using **endurance** in a phrase of positive self-talk:

"I have endurance. When I have a goal that is important to me, I do not quit. No matter what obstacles I have to deal with or overcome, I will not stop, I will not give up, and I will not give in. I have endurance."

Chapter 8

The Secret Words for
The Top Ten Mental Skills

It's important to keep in mind that the purpose of focusing on the secret words is not just to know what they are; it is to make them a part of your own mental programming—the kind that helps you shape your thinking in a positive way. Beyond just reading through the words, it is when you become completely familiar with them, that they become wired in, and they play a part in how you think, and how you deal with each day.

This chapter's list of secret words is a good example. It is a list of words that should be taught in schools. It's hard to imagine anyone becoming super-successful in life without them. And yet, not one of the words in this chapter is about career or wealth or position. They are about the *inside* you—the part of you that makes everything else work.

You can have the greatest education or experience or talents, but without the mental skills that are outlined below, the biggest part of your internal success tools would be missing. Without the skills of *optimism, creativity, courage, patience, perseverance,* and the other secret words covered in this chapter, you cannot become the individual you would become by having them.

63. Optimism

The first word on our list of mental skills is *optimism.* This word is a cousin of the word *positive,* and lives next door to the words *faith* and *belief.*

For success people, optimism is their default way of looking at life. It expresses a worldview that sees the glass as half *full.* It says that things *work*, no matter how great the challenge, and that behind the darkest cloud there is always a silver lining.

Studies in the field of neuroscience show that because of the way the brain is programmed, practicing an attitude of *optimism* actually wires your brain to deal with problems in a more positive way. It helps you confront the problem, find solutions, and take action—the same exact qualities that help a person become successful.

People who practice optimism have more successful days, precisely because optimism affects virtually everything about them— their attitude, their belief in being able to deal with difficulties and overcome odds, their creativity in exploring solutions, their openness to opportunities, and their overall outlook on life as they go through each day.

It should also be noted that a proper mindset of optimism does not ignore the difficulties and the negative realities of life. Quite the opposite. A mindset of optimism is simply more capable of dealing with problems and overcoming them. It recognizes problems for what they are, and deals with them.

An interesting, and telling, side note on the value of optimism is that a meta-analysis of nearly 300,000 people showed that individuals who have a high level of optimism had a 35% lower risk of major heart complications, such as a cardiac death, stroke, or heart attack, compared to the pessimists in each of the studies. That's another great (and sobering) reason why having a mental state of optimism is not only essential to your well-being—it can also be a very healthy thing to do.

* * *

*Why **optimism** matters:*

Optimism wins; pessimism loses. The rise of optimism is one of humankind's greatest blessings. Its positive effects are spiritual, mental, emotional, and physical—that is, our optimism affects everything about us. Having optimism is among the most effective means of dealing with anything in which your attitude plays a role. Once you've experienced optimism—and practiced it as a significant part of your attitude each day—it is impossible to imagine the vacuum that would be created by living without it. A mindset of *optimism* is one of the greatest success generators you can have.

* * *

Using **optimism** in a phrase of positive self-talk:

"I have an attitude of optimism, and I choose to see life in a positive way. I am very practical and realistic, but I know that the more I believe in the best—and work to achieve it—the more of the best comes my way."

64. Creativity

The word *creativity* carries a message so powerful, so rich with possibilities for everyone, that it is taught to pre-schoolers and college students alike. There is a good reason why creativity is so important: *'creativity' is the beginning of everything.*

Creativity gives you—from within your own mind—the chance to *make*, or *improve*, or *change*, or *rearrange*, or *fix*, or *invent*, or *modify*, or *explore* an unlimited number of revelations that make up the world you live in. Creativity lets you see that world as a world of *endless possibilities*.

Creativity isn't just for children; it's for everyone who wants to play in the infinite sandbox of life.

* * *

*Why **creativity** matters:*
It is *creativity* that allows us to become greater than our physical selves. Creativity is the transcendent expression of our minds that causes us to rise above our otherwise

earthly limitations. To be able to create something from thought only, and turn it into touchable reality, or to bring forth from a single mind, endless expression—like the soul-embracing passages of beautiful music— is a gift that seems more than human. And yet the gift of *creativity* is there, within each of us, every day, anytime we want to call upon it, and bring it to life. *Creativity* is our connection to the perfect artistry of the unlimited universe we live in.

* * *

Using **creativity** in a phrase of positive self-talk:

"I am creative. I practice seeing things in new and different ways. I'm good at finding new ideas and great solutions, because I am creative."

65. Courage

Courage is something we call upon when we believe the challenge we face is greater than the resources we have to overcome it. Courage is not a lack of fear in the face of adversity—it is the determination to overcome the adversity in spite of the fear.

To have courage does not require that you have the experience of years, or the benefit of wisdom; even a young child, facing death, can have it. Courage requires that you bring to life an inner strength which transcends your fear—and urges you forward in spite of it.

Your choice to have courage, even when things look bleak or your back is against the wall, can bring to life strengths within you that you didn't know you possessed. Most successful people will tell you that there were times when courage was all they had left— but it was because of their courage that they survived. And all of them would agree that they have overcome far more obstacles *with* courage—than without it.

*   *   *

*Why **courage** matters:*

Courage is an expression of the human spirit at its finest. It is a noble thing—an inner strength that stands taller than the challenge that stands against it. Often, it is not the giant of a person who displays the greatest courage—it is the weaker, more vulnerable among us. Our own personal courage may not be known to us. Although we suspect that one day our courage will be tested, few of us know how much of it we have until we are called upon to have it.

* * *

Using **courage** in a phrase of positive self-talk:

"I know that having courage is a choice, and I choose to have courage. I stand strong. I have courage. And I go forward with the determination and the inner strength to rise above any challenge I face."

66. Patience

Patience is a sign of wisdom—which is why it is seldom practiced by children. Patience can be learned and practiced, and with enough practice, you can perfect it.

In a classic martial arts film, karate icon Bruce Lee, when thrown to the bottom of an elevator shaft with no means of escape, evaluates his situation, and then calmly sits down in the lotus position, breathes deeply and slowly, and goes to sleep. It is a perfect depiction of practicing the art of patience. If more people learned to do that—in their minds—there would be fewer arguments, fewer mistakes, and less pain in the world.

The amount of patience you exercise today is determined almost entirely by the amount of "patience programs" that have been wired into your brain. That means your patience, or how much of it you practice, is a habit.

Actively practicing patience and using the right self-talk can change the wiring of your brain and make you more patient. Since your level of patience plays a huge role in your success in relationships, in your work, in your self-esteem, in your health, in your ability to reach goals, and in your peace of mind, having *more* patience without having to grow old to get it is a good idea.

And if you become a master at having patience, I'm sure Bruce Lee would have been proud of you.

* * *

*Why **patience** matters:*
Patience is one of the most helpful and practical habits you can have. Having a patience mindset does wonders for reducing anxiety and lowering the levels of stress hormones in your body. But as important as those benefits are, an even greater benefit of having a mindset of patience is that it elevates you to a higher level of thinking— more aware of the moment, more self-controlled. Practicing patience keeps you mindful of the 'bigger picture'—your greater purpose and goals—and helps you avoid making unnecessary mistakes. While you're staying calm, seeing the moment in a measured, self-confident way, your peace of

mind, and the clarity of your awareness, goes *up*—and your errors go *down*.

*   *   *

Using **patience** in a phrase of positive self-talk:

"I have patience. I'm good at having patience, because I practice having it. Having patience allows me to think things through, understand more, see things clearly, and give time the chance to pass. I have patience."

67. Perseverance

Along with its three sister words—*persistence, tenacity,* and *endurance*—perseverance is one of the essential skills of achievement.

Perseverance means to *"stay with it, no matter what."* It is both a choice and an attitude. When it comes to reaching goals, big or small, the people who refuse to give up do better than people who drop out or stop trying. To find out if you need to work on having more perseverance, you only need to ask yourself one question: *"Do I give up and give in, or do I refuse to quit—and win?"*

The more difficult it is to reach the goal, the more perseverance you need to stay with it. Knowing that, helps. Because you can allow yourself to stop when the going gets tough—or, like the self-talk below, you can say, *"I'm not stopping. I'm not giving up or giving in. I have perseverance!"* In dealing with any challenge, your chance of winning can turn on that one, simple choice alone.

* * *

*Why **perseverance** matters:*

There is a great advantage in having perseverance; it allows you to overcome many obstacles just by waiting them out. Clearly, perseverance is a choice, but a choice that is best made consciously, so that not giving up becomes a tactical, planned for, element of your life strategy. In time, with practice, perseverance becomes a 'wired in' part of your mental software. When that happens, being *"someone who never gives up"* becomes one of your assets, and a positive part of the description of your character.

*   *   *

Using **perseverance** in a phrase of positive self-talk:

"I'm not stopping. I'm not giving up or giving in. I have perseverance! When I have something I want to make happen in my life, I go for it, I make it happen, and I do not give up. I have perseverance!"

68. Integrity

For the person who wants to be successful, the most important meaning of the word 'integrity' is to be *integrated*. It is to have all of you—the mental, emotional, spiritual and physical aspects of you—working together. The truly integrated person is someone who is living a life that is in balance, having *all* of your facets—both internal and external—working in harmony.

That's why the ideas of *integrity* and *honesty* are so often found together; if you are a person of integrity, you would also be a person of honesty. It is your integrity—the complete integration of all of the important parts of your life—that creates your honesty.

* * *

*Why **integrity** matters:*
You are defined in part by the amount of integrity you bring to anything. Integrity is an intangible mindset that has tangible or observable results; when you have integrity, it is a part of your character, and it shows. Integrity is a badge of honor. It identifies you

as someone who has principles, that there is a sense of strong moral conviction to how you think and how you interact with life. To be a person of quality, a mindset of integrity is essential. There is no greatness, and no true fulfillment in life without it.

* * *

Using *integrity* in a phrase of positive self-talk:

"I have integrity. I keep all areas of my life mentally, emotionally, physically, and spiritually integrated, in harmony, and in balance at all times. I have integrity."

69. Heart

Heart is one of the core words of this book. That's because this quality of *heart*, this deep strength of the human heart, when added to the other attributes we're discussing, gives more strength to all of them.

Having heart is caring, it requires strength, it is often selfless, and it is the essence of empathy. But heart is even more than that; it's deeper than that.

People who have *heart* have more endurance—they stay with the task longer. They have more depth of feeling for whoever it is they are helping or whatever it is they are doing. And they often sacrifice something in the process, so having *heart* is not always an easy thing to do.

The kind of heart we're talking about is that amazing 'something' *within* people that causes them to sacrifice, gives them courage, overrides personal need, and ends up making them heroes among humans.

Think about *heart*, and what it means to you—and how much of it you have. If you take some time and think about this, you will probably come up with a good answer. That way, when the time comes for you to have heart, in the deepest, most meaningful way, you'll know you have what it takes, you're in the right place, and you're doing the right thing.

* * *

*Why **heart** matters:*

To *not* have heart would be to live out only a small part of the person you were born to be. It would be living only as a dim shadow of who you could be, the complete, powerful, loving, caring being you were meant to be. Heart is the living essence of your spiritual good. *Having* heart expresses that essence. The more of it you have, the greater the depth of your humanity, and the greater your strength as an individual. Heart is the amount of strong, caring, courageous, selfless spirit you bring to your life.

* * *

Using *heart* in a phrase of positive self-talk:

"I have heart. I care deeply, I help others, and I choose high mountains to climb. Instead of worrying about my own sacrifice, I am content to know that I am blessed to be here, choosing to help, and determined to succeed."

70. Strength

Strength: Everyone wants it, many people fear it, some people have more of it than others, and life seems to work better when you have enough of it.

For the success person, *strength* is your ability to remain stable—to defend yourself—against any and all of life's challenges. There are different kinds of strength: there is physical strength, mental strength, emotional strength, and spiritual strength.

But if you want to have true, personal strength, to those I would add a few more—some of the greatest strengths of all: strength of *purpose*, strength of *character* and strength of *will*.

I won't suggest that you can suddenly have every kind of strength just by deciding to have them. Like building strength in muscles, to have strength of any kind, you have to exercise—and you have to practice getting strong. That won't give you more strength overnight, but I believe readers of this book who think about the strengths they would like to have, will set a goal to attain them.

*   *   *

Why **strength** *matters:*
It is strength that allows us to stand tall––in our bodies and in our minds. Without a mindset of strength, we can easily give way to victimhood—allowing our fears or the world around us to determine our vulnerabilities for us—whether they are real or imagined. *Strength,* in our terms here, means that you take responsibility for yourself, and you determine what you are strong enough to undertake or overcome. Your strength is governed by the stature of your mind and spirit, the places from which your strength originates.

*   *   *

Using **strength** in a phrase of positive self-talk:

"I am strong in many ways. I have strength of spirit, strength of character, and strength of will. I know the path I choose to follow, and I have the strength to reach my goal."

71. Will

Your *will* is a force within you that determines the level of your personal resolution to succeed or overcome—no matter what the obstacle may be.

Some parts of *will* may be inborn, and come from your genetic coding. But the greatest part of will is born of creating a sense of *self*—through hard-won life lessons that teach you the value of standing strong, bending with the wind, but always surviving.

To have *will*, you have to practice *self-determination*. (No one can do that for you.) To do that, you have to think for yourself, be willing to stand your ground, face the challenges that will ultimately strengthen you, and in the end, give you the mental armor that nothing can defeat.

Being a person of strong will gives you a distinction that stands higher than almost all other distinctions. The lowliest of paupers, with the strongest of wills, stands taller than the king who has less.

* * *

*Why **will** matters:*
The core of one's will lies in a personal determination to overcome any chosen challenge, no matter how difficult it may be. Will is, in part, a result of how you define your limits and boundaries—which of them you accept, and which you don't. Will never comes from a life of ease; it comes from overcoming continuing challenges—you against the world—which creates a lasting determination to survive, and to win.

* * *

Using **will** in a phrase of positive self-talk:

"My will is strong. It is alive within me, and it grows stronger every day. I willingly meet any challenge I face. I work to overcome it, I learn from it, and my will grows stronger because of it."

72. Resilience

The coaching cliche' says it's not how often you get knocked down that counts—it's how often you get back up. That's true; that is *resilience*, but success people take resilience an important step further.

Success people see defeats, setbacks, and recoveries as *a natural part of the process of achievement*. They expect challenges. They anticipate them. They plan for them. And when the challenges come, not only are they ready for them—they consider nothing less than overcoming them.

That means resilience is a *mindset*. And because it's a mindset, it is another of the skills you can practice having.

Resilience is a way of looking at life in which you never consider giving up just because things get tough. Instead of allowing a problem to stop you, you automatically shift into resilience, immediately take the steps you need to take to overcome the problem— and move on. No complaints, no blame, no negative attitude, and no energy lost. You just get back up, dust yourself off, smile, and keep going. That's resilience.

* * *

*Why **resilience** matters:*
The opposite of a mindset of resilience is the habit of quitting—or stopping too soon—because life, at the moment, is uncomfortable, or seems unfair, or is just difficult. Like any great achievement, living a fully-accomplished life takes *grit*, and that requires an enduring force of *resilience*. This quality can be mustered at will, but in time, resilience becomes a mindset, which is a habit, which in turn becomes a way of life.

* * *

Using **resilience** in a phrase of positive self-talk:

"I am resilient! I practice making resilience a natural part of my life every day. When I face a setback of any kind, I deal with it, I overcome it, I learn from it, and I move on."

Chapter 9

The Secret Words for
Creating a Success Mindset

The secret words in this chapter identify the qualities that create a foundation for 'success thinking.' That foundation is made up of the deep programs the right words create in the brain. And it is those programs that separate how successful people look at life, from people who live below the success level.

The objective is to give your mind the same kinds of foundational programs that success people have in common.

Even if you haven't been super-focused specifically on these concepts up to now (they are usually thought of only passively), you can still learn them, focus on them now, and make them a part of your strongest programs.

We'll begin with a secret word that is inherent in all personal growth, and that all success people make a friend of. The word is *change.*

NOTE: To download the free user tools—*The Secret Words Workbook, The Secret Words Poster, Six Weeks to Success* home coaching program, and *Personal Goal-Setting Forms*—see Chapter 12, or go to:
www.thesecretwordsofsuccess.com/tools

---

73. Change

Change is something that many people are wary of. With too *little* change, we live in stasis, and go nowhere. With too *much* change, we become confused and insecure. But success people have learned to see change from a different perspective. To them, the secret to mastering change is to focus on finding the positive benefits that hide within it.

How do you view change? How does it make you feel? Do you welcome it? Do you control change, or does change control you? People who learn to master dealing with change recognize that not only is *positive change* necessary and welcome, it is also essential for progression through life. The secret, for them, is learning to see change as a natural part of the way things are.

Success people make the choice to create change when it is necessary, accept it when acceptance is the only option, understand it, never fear it, make it a friend, and find within it the opportunity to grow.

* * *

*Why **change** matters:*
A mindset that embraces change will do
better for you than having a mindset that
fights it. With an open, receptive mindset,
you view change as a natural and often
necessary part of the circumstances of life.
Instead of expending negative energy
fighting change, with a mindset that finds
the positive in change you will wisely spend
the same energy turning change to your
advantage, and finding ways to excel because
of it.

* * *

Using **change** in a phrase of positive self-
talk:

*"I welcome positive change in my life. I
know that in order to grow, I also need to
accept change as a natural part of my
journey. So I welcome the change, and I am
thankful for the growth it brings to my life."*

74. Belief

The power of *belief* is one of the most helpful life forces you will ever possess.

One kind of belief comes from *knowing*, and it is based on learning, experience, and reason—which means this kind of belief comes primarily from programs that have been wired into your brain.

The other kind of belief—the kind that is also practiced by success people—is an energy that is yours the moment you choose to have it. At any time, for any reason, *you can choose to believe.* And when you do, the more you practice having belief, the more powerful it becomes.

An example of this kind of belief is when you are working at reaching a goal, and in spite of your efforts you don't know how things will turn out. So, along with doing everything on your list to make your goal happen, you also decide to *believe* that you'll reach the goal. In this case, the belief itself may be as important as the action steps you're taking to reach the goal.

Belief can have a spiritual or a metaphysical component, but you don't have to believe in those qualities for belief to work for you. Choosing to have belief, especially strong, willful belief, triggers unconscious support programs in your brain that help you do what is necessary to bring the object of your belief to life. So, strong belief creates a self-fulfilling prophecy. The *belief*, itself, helps create the *result*.

Your decision to believe sets up your mental state and defines your determination to find the necessary solutions, keep taking action, stay with it until the job is done, and succeed.

Without belief, dreams and ideas falter and fail. *With* belief, dreams and ideas come to life. Choose belief. Practice belief. Keep doing it. And then watch what happens.

* * *

*Why **belief** matters:*
The alternative to having a mindset of *belief* is most often one of passive acceptance—leaving the outcome up to fate.

Or worse, you could have a mindset of *disbelief*—a way of thinking that will almost certainly doom your efforts to failure. But, when you choose to have a *mindset of belief*, something wonderful happens! You define your intention, you decide to have faith in the outcome, and you proceed as though your belief will come to pass—and the results *change* because you made that choice. There is an almost magical quality in doing that. You choose to believe, and your belief changes the results.

* * *

Using **belief** in a phrase of positive self-talk:

"I have belief. I choose to believe, and I'm good at it. When I choose to believe in something, I do everything I need to do to make what I believe in come to life. I have belief, and I believe in the best."

75. Brave

Brave is a word that combines *strength*, *courage*, and *character*. The reason for choosing to be brave is that life is often tough, or difficult, or terrifying—and being brave is one of the best ways we have learned to rise above the problems we face, survive in spite of them, and even excel.

When life is overwhelming, and you can't see a way though it, sometimes the one thing you *can* do is to be brave. That's a good choice to make. When you choose to be brave—to override your fear, survive, believe in the future, and just keep breathing, no matter what—things almost always get better.

Another time bravery is called for is when you decide to take a stand for something you believe in. In these times, when nearly everything people once believed in is being called into question, it takes courage and a brave heart to stand up for what you know to be truth—especially when that truth is not what is popular at the moment.

Success people choose truth, but when they are called upon to defend that truth, they bring to bear a number of the qualities we are discussing in this book. Among these are *will, courage, heart,* and *determination.* And, of course, they also have to be *brave.*

* * *

*Why **brave** matters:*

Bravery is universally admired; collectively we feel safer and more secure when bravery is present. As an individual, choosing to be brave immediately heightens your stature. It brings up reserves of strength and courage from within you—and brings to life the true nature of your spirit. To be brave is a high ideal. It is both a measure of who you are as a person, and also a reminder of the remarkable qualities a human being can possess.

* * *

Using **brave** in a phrase of positive self-talk:

"I choose to be brave. No matter what happens, I have the strength to deal with it, and the determination to rise above it. The more I practice being brave, the stronger, the braver, and the more capable I become."

76. Can

What an amazingly simple, but powerful, word this is! One word, of just three letters, defines the difference between those who *do* and those who *don't*. The more often you replace the word *can't* with the word *can*, the greater your chance of doing well in anything you do.

The reason the word *can* is so important is that it defines an essential part of who you are, what you believe about yourself, what you think you can accomplish, and what you will actually achieve.

When you precede the word *can* with the word *'I'*—to make it *'I can'*—you tap into a force from deep within your mind that will help you accomplish anything possible you want to achieve. There is no word on my list that is more important than the word *can*.

* * *

Why **can** *matters:*
Can is the watchword of one of the most powerful and worthwhile mindsets you can

have. *Can* is the embodiment of positive belief, and the foundation of a winning attitude. The opposite of 'can' is 'cannot'—which declares a predetermined acceptance of defeat. How much better it is to place the word *can* at the top of our list—as we step forward into our days, and fight the good fight that is the nature of our life.

*   *   *

Using ***can*** in a phrase of positive self-talk:

"I believe in myself. Instead of doubting myself, or telling myself what I cannot accomplish, I choose to use the self-talk that says, I can, I can, I can."

77. Freedom

True freedom is the opportunity for your spirit to soar without limitation. It is the opportunity to breathe for yourself. It is the right to make your choices for yourself.

When your spirit lives in freedom, it means you get to have control over your life. But there is a price: in order to have real freedom, you have to be willing to take responsibility for yourself. And that means that the achievement of your goals is up to you. The circumstances of your life—even day to day—are up to you.

When you exercise personal freedom, how you deal with anything is up to you. How much joy and happiness you have is up to you. And your overall success in life is up to you. You create it; you live it, and you *own* it.

That's a lot of responsibility, but that's what real freedom gives you. That doesn't mean you have to do everything on your own. But having real freedom *does* mean that you are not a victim of the world around you. It means the *opposite*: it means *you* choose to set your spirit free—and be in control of your life.

*   *   *

*Why **freedom** matters:*
Freedom is the opposite of limitation. We all have limitations, of course. But, the less our limitations impair us, the more freedom we have to spread our wings and fly—to soar to greater heights and become the 'unlimited' beings we were born to be. The greatest impairment to our freedom is within our own minds: we bind our spirits with *doubt, disbelief, hesitation,* and *fear*. A spirit bound is a spirit lost. A spirit that finds *freedom* is a spirit that soars.

*   *   *

Using **freedom** in a phrase of positive self-talk:

"I choose freedom. I choose to soar. I choose to be responsible for every breath I take, every step I take, and everything I do with this incredible life I have been given. I move past my own doubt, disbelief, hesitation, and fear. I choose freedom, and I make my life work."

78. Responsibility

The first meaning of personal responsibility is that you are accountable for *you*, and you don't demand that others do your *living* for you, your *thinking* for you, or your *breathing* for you. It is when you recognize that most of 'what is to be' in your life is ultimately up to you. Responsibility is a foundation stone of good character—which is the bedrock of a quality life.

The deeper meaning of the word *responsibility* is how well you *respond* to the life you're living right now. This takes you beyond the common meaning of responsibility to your job, your family, your schooling, or the routine expectations placed on you by everyday life. It actually sets up how well you do at anything you do.

Some people don't quite get it, and never fully respond to their life in a way that makes it work. Other people learn that they have a chance to respond to life, to be *responsible*— and to get it *right*, as often as possible—day after day.

To success people, being *responsible* means 'responding to the life you're living' in its entirety—being fully accountable, and making your life work.

*　*　*

*Why **responsibility** matters:*

The opposite of a mindset of responsibility is a lack of accountability—a passive mindset that leads to chaos (and with chaos, nothing works well). In order to have a mindset that includes it, responsibility has to be learned, and then practiced. Once learned, responsibility overrides chaos—as well as laxity and an attitude of victimhood. It replaces fear of living with a sense of positive anticipation. Having responsibility is being accountable for all of the values and actions that make up your life. It is so thoroughly enabling and life enhancing, that *responsibility* is its own reward.

*　*　*

Using **responsibility** in a phrase of positive self-talk:

"I take responsibility for myself. I take care of my life in every positive way. I think for myself, speak for myself, believe for myself, and act for myself. And I am responsible for everything I do in my life."

79. Hope

Hope is a gift. To be able to *hope* is one of those special, mysterious gifts we have been given from the universe itself. Even though we create hope entirely in our imagination, *with* it we have endured more, outlasted more, and accomplished more than we ever would have without it.

Along with *belief* and *faith*, *hope* is one of the most powerful tools we have when we are faced with both our own fallibility and our potential for failure.

Having *hope* suggests the promise of something better—the greater tomorrow, finding the solution to the problem, the possibility of overcoming the toughest odds— and coming through it all and still be alive and breathing.

Hope is one of the strongest armaments we have when everything else has failed us. People who lose hope are destined to lose the battle. But people who refuse to let go of hope often *turn* the tide of the battle and win. That is a remarkable power for something that we cannot touch or see. And it reminds us to never underestimate the strength of the human spirit.

* * *

*Why **hope** matters:*

A mindset that is without hope is hope*less*. It views the world—and the future—as, ultimately, a losing game. A lack of hope drains the emotions of positive energy, and gives way to the acceptance of predetermined failure. But, an active *mindset of hope* stands against the parade of life's problems. It doesn't blindly rely on wishful thinking—it shines the positive light of possibility on adversity, and creates an attitude of *solving* problems instead of giving in to them. *Hope* is a blessing that helps us endure—while we practice getting better and stronger.

* * *

Using *hope* in a phrase of positive self-talk:

"I always have hope. Because I do, when I'm doing something I believe in that counts, I refuse to give up or give in. I have faith. I have belief. And I have hope."

80. Balance

Balance is something most people have to work at achieving—but finding it is always a positive. Choosing to have a balanced life helps you live each day in a more calm, measured way.

To work well, all parts of life require balance: your relationships, your work, your health, your activities—all of these work best when they are all in balance, and balanced with each other.

Balance is created by the amount of *time*, *effort*, and *mental focus* you apply to each of the many things you do. The more you are in control of those, the more balance you have, and the more control you have in your life.

Success people make a point of maintaining proper balance because doing so helps to ensure that they are placing their energies on the right priorities—while they keep themselves operating and living in the smoothest possible way.

* * *

*Why **balance** matters:*

A mindset of balance creates even-handedness in your day. It oversees a proper distribution of your mental and physical effort—never allotting too much or too little to each entry on the list of things that vie for your attention. The circumstances of the day will often, by themselves, put things out of balance—and few days are perfect. But when you maintain a mindset of *balance*, you will have a regulator—like the pendulum of a clock—that helps keep you centered.

* * *

Using **balance** in a phrase of positive self-talk:

"I choose to create balance in my life every day. I am always mindful of the amount of time, effort and focus I invest in anything I do. Because I create balance in what I do each day, I create positive control in my life."

81. Happiness

Happiness is a sense of well-being that tells us that, at least for the moment, something is *right* with the world. It is another mindset that is a choice. Everyone wants to have happiness—and yet many people never realize they can choose to have it.

The important thing to know about happiness is that it is a habit. People who think *positive* are happier than people who think *negative*. That's because they practice using positive self-talk, and their self-talk determines how they feel about life—so they are practicing being happy.

This is something you can try for yourself at any time. In the middle of your day, pause for a moment, and say, *"I choose to be happy, right now."* The more you do that, the more the message will overcome the darkness, get wired in, adjust the chemistry of your brain, and improve the brightness of your day.

* * *

*Why **happiness** matters:*

Happiness—having a heightened sense of positive well-being—is not only a worthwhile goal, it is essential to a balanced life. Some would argue that finding and holding onto happiness is not a worthwhile pursuit; they would say it is not attainable, or it does not last. But the degree to which happiness is attainable is determined by the mindset of the person who pursues it. And that means that happiness is not only a mindset; it is a choice.

*   *   *

Using **happiness** in a phrase of positive self-talk:

"I choose to be happy. I can look at life, and anything in it, any way I choose to see it. And right now, I choose to be happy."

82. Harmony

Life's game is that it sends us chaos and disorder—and waits for us to turn them into peace and harmony. But what a wonderful thing it is when we get it right! When the difficulties of daily life are replaced by the perfect blend of musical notes, the colors of a rainbow after a storm, or the beaming smile or warm embrace of a loved one—that's when we know harmony is winning.

Just as the acceptance of chaos and disorder can be a habit, so can the pursuit of harmony become a habit—and a much healthier, more pleasant one.

When you look for it, you find there is harmony everywhere in life, every day. The more you take note of it, the more it becomes a part of your thoughts, and creates a mindset that attracts it. There is harmony in music and beauty and art, of course. But there is also harmony in agreement, in making the day go right, in working together with others, in the life-giving richness of a good relationship, in living life in a way that has a sense of 'rightness.'

When you ask yourself the question, "How is the harmony in my life today?" or "What can I do to create more harmony and peace of mind in my life today?" listen for your thoughts—for your answers. They will tell you if there's work to be done.

Harmony is the perfect balance you feel when you know you have turned what could have been the ordinary chaos of life into the beautiful notes of a well-orchestrated symphony—a day well lived.

* * *

*Why **harmony** matters:*
Creating harmony is essential to a sense of well-being—one of the primary attributes of true success. Since there cannot be success without well-being, and there cannot be well-being without harmony, practicing having a *mindset* of harmony is a major step toward becoming a success person.

* * *

Using *harmony* in a phrase of positive self-talk:

"I bring harmony and well-being into my life every day. I know that calm, peace of mind, and contentment are the result of the harmony I find, and the harmony I create."

Chapter 10

The Secret Words for
A Day in Your Life

If for one typical day, you could look into the mind of a success person—someone who has their life completely together—what would you see? What would they be thinking? What would their attitude be? *What kind of software would their brain be using?*

And, if you looked into your own mind on an average day, what would you see? What would your software be? Would your thoughts be similar to the success person's thoughts, or would they be different?

The power of the secret words in this chapter is that they give you insight into the

235

kinds of things success people think about most often—even every day. If you could see into the mind of a success person for a day, you would *not* find a focus on *fear*, or being a *victim*, or *poverty*, or *lack of potential*, or *failure*.

Instead, you would find the success person focusing on *potential, opportunity, promise, prosperity, positive risk, reward, achievement, true wealth, home,* and *success.*

As we explore the words below, ask yourself how many of them find their way into your own thoughts each day. And then, make it a goal to master each of them, and own them for life.

83. Potential

The idea of *potential* is so popular with success-oriented people that, in the last century, a name given to the personal growth field was 'the human potential movement.' Since that time, studies in neuroscience have shone a spotlight on the important role a person's thoughts and attitudes play in the life-long wiring of the individual's brain.

We now know there is a clear, neurological, brain-wiring link between having a 'success attitude' and creating long-term personal growth. And we know that wanting to live up to your *potential* is not wishful thinking. It is attainable through taking practical, ongoing steps that are based on solid brain science.

If reaching more of your potential is important to you, the most important of those ongoing steps is to make sure you wire your brain in the right way—the most positive, healthy way possible. That means always using the best possible self-talk you can wire into your brain.

* * *

*Why **potential** matters:*
The mindset that fails to recognize *potential* is the mindset that takes a pass on the exceptional opportunities life presents—it is sitting out the game instead of playing the game and doing your best to win. But a mindset that recognizes potential is better prepared—it is aware of the opportunities life has to offer. It is the recognition of your potential that shows you the incredible possibilities that are in store for you—the moment you accept the quest to seek them out.

* * *

Using **potential** in a phrase of positive self-talk:

"I make sure I am doing what I need to do to live up to my potential. I like who I am today, and I can't wait to see who I'm going to be tomorrow."

84. Opportunity

Opportunity is what some people see—when other people see only challenges. To the positive, aware person, the world is *filled* with opportunity. Seeing the opportunities that are there is one of the results of training yourself to think in the positive. It is in life's challenges that the seeds of opportunity are most often planted. And it is when you see life in the positive that you recognize the opportunities, focus in on them, and bring them to life.

Opportunity is anything useful that can be created by serendipity, or from any challenge or situation you face. Instead of the rushing river causing the traveler to end his journey, the success person sees the river as the opportunity to build a bridge. People who think in the negative see problems and impossible obstacles everywhere. People who practice thinking in the positive see *opportunity*.

*   *   *

*Why **opportunity** matters:*

Not having an *opportunity mindset* can cause you to miss out on some of the most rewarding experiences of life. It is when you choose to have a mindset that seeks out opportunity—and looks *forward* to it—that you begin to discover the positive side of any challenge, and recognize the chance to turn any situation into something that makes things better. Those who see opportunity as positive potential, experience life more completely than those who avoid the promise of the unknown, or fail to see opportunity for what it is—a rich storehouse of endless possibilities.

*   *   *

Using **opportunity** in a phrase of positive self-talk:

"I deal with challenges by finding the positive opportunities they hold within them. I am always practical and realistic, but when I deal with a challenge, I see it as an opportunity, and turn it into a win."

85. Promise

You have unlimited promise and potential. Right now. That's not wishful thinking; that's a promise you were born with. No one is born to fail. We are all born to succeed. It doesn't make any difference how difficult life has been, or what challenges have come your way; your *promise* never goes away. Your potential is never taken from you. You still have all of the promise you were born to live out.

Success people understand *promise*. That's why they can suffer defeats and endure hardships, but still go on, seeing each day as a new opportunity. Challenges educate them and make them stronger; but challenges don't take their promise away.

A good way to look at your promise is to see it as a gift that cannot be taken from you. It is a gift that was given to you; problems and defeats can't take it away, and failure doesn't lessen it.

Your promise is still there. It has endless patience. And it is waiting for you.

*   *   *

*Why **promise** matters:*

A promise mindset is defined by the question, *"Am I fulfilling my promise today?"* Doing that—fulfilling your promise—can be achieved in many ways. The simplest measure of your success is whether or not you are growing, each day. If you are growing, you are probably fulfilling your promise—or at least, working at it. It may be that no one quite lives up to the promise and the potential they had at the moment of their birth. But clearly, if you work at it—if you choose to practice having an active *promise mindset*—you have a far greater probability of living up to your best, than if you did nothing about it, or passively left your *promise* up to *chance*.

*   *   *

Using *promise* in a phrase of positive self-talk:

"I was born with promise, and it is with me, still. I am mindful, every day, of the opportunities I have to live up to my promise. My promise will never leave me, and I will never abandon my promise."

86. Prosperity

Prosperity, as it is thought of by success people, means much more than financial wealth. Merriam-Webster gets this right when they list *19* synonyms for prosperity, and they accurately include riches that include *abundance, fitness, healthiness, robustness, soundness,* and *wholesomeness,* among them. Prosperity means *an abundance of good.*

If your mind lives in poverty, so will you. It's not surprising, then, that instead of seeing themselves struggling through a life of failure, hardship, and adversity, success people think about their lives in a completely different way; along with *opportunity* and *potential*, they think *prosperity*.

Because your thoughts set up your reality, it's a good idea to make *prosperity* a dominant thought pattern—one of the stronger programs in your brain. If what you think about most is what you're likely to get most, you might as well fill your mind with thoughts that lead to an abundance of good.

*   *   *

*Why **prosperity** matters:*
What is significant about a prosperity mindset is that people who are raised *without* it perpetuate the condition. A *mindset* that lacks prosperity creates a *life* that lacks prosperity. You can, however, by your own *choice*, create a prosperity mindset, and practice having it. With the right self-talk, the right conditioning, you can rewire how your brain views prosperity. In doing that, you are changing your brain's perception of your own identity to one who deserves the goodness of life—from *'has not,'* to *'has.'*

*   *   *

Using **prosperity** in a phrase of positive self-talk:

"I have a prosperity mindset. I see my world as being filled with abundance and prosperity. And because I see prosperity in my mind, I do what it takes to make it happen in my life."

87. Risk

To the success person, 'risk' is a *positive* word. Risk, carefully evaluated and entered into, is often the deciding feature of a success. But while many ventures in life—whether personal or professional—involve risk, it's how you personally *view* risk that will give you the advantage.

Perhaps the most important message about risk is that people who don't take risks don't *live*—not in the alive, aware, courageous sense of living. Instead of venturing into the sunlight, where all of their growth could come from, they stay in the shadows, and cower in the darkness. That's not always their fault. They were programmed—wired—usually from a young age, to *fear* risk, instead of *understanding* it and *using* it, as they venture outward into the great unknowns of life.

The best way to view the idea of risk is to do so with *study* and with *courage*. *Studying* the risk carefully will keep you somewhat safer, and minimize your chances of failure. *Courage* will get you to take a deep breath, square your shoulders, nod your head *yes*, step forward, and make it work.

*   *   *

*Why **risk** matters:*

Without a positive risk mindset, there is no forward progress. In the course of daily activities, one of the meanings of 'risk-averse' is 'one who lacks confidence.' That is a sign of someone who is not likely to excel. Fortunately, even the most courageous person can also be practical; risk is not an all-or-nothing proposition, and each day can call for a different level of caution or confidence. The winning mindset is the one that is willing to take the risk, when *risk* is what is called for.

*   *   *

Using *risk* in a phrase of positive self-talk:

"I see risk as a positive, necessary step forward for many good things in my life. I carefully study and learn—to understand anything I need to know about the risk that is in front of me. Once I see the right path, I step forward with courage, determination, and the joy of moving onward and upward in my life."

88. Reward

Reward is is one of the grades you get on life's report card—the positive result of doing something well. It is a way to recognize what you've done right—so you can take note of it——and do it right again.

You also get to reward *yourself*—a positive idea that is often used by success people. You can even write the reward into your goal plan, and set yourself up for an emotionally viable trophy when the goal is met.

Sometimes you don't get to choose the rewards you will receive. But it's important to recognize them when they come. Whether it's the dinner, the applause, the thank you, the bronze plaque, the gift, the check, the hug, or just the way you smiled when you looked at yourself in the mirror when you got the job done—*recognize the reward*. It's a sign that life is working, and you're doing another thing right.

Another kind of reward is the one that is synonymous with 'blessing'—the kind of feeling you get when all is right with the world, and life is its own reward.

* * *

*Why **reward** matters:*

Reward is on the list of success words because, for many, it is a powerful motivator. Depending on your outlook, reward could be profits, a bonus, recognition, a promotion, a trophy, or a host of other benefits you can earn in a material world. Or, to you, reward might take the form of recognizing the results of something you've done well, or seeing someone benefit because of your efforts. Or your reward could be just knowing you're living in a way that is aligned with your purpose. But in each case, your *rewards* are the result of the *actions* you take. They are signposts—reminders—that tell you how to get things right.

* * *

Using **reward** in a phrase of positive self-talk:

"Every reward, of any kind, is a message to me—that I'm on track, in tune, in touch, and going for it! I enjoy the goal, I enjoy the work, I enjoy the journey, and I enjoy the reward. With rewards as my signposts, I learn what I'm doing right—and how to make my life even better."

89. Achievement

A mindset of *achievement* plays an important role in the lives of all success people. For them, achievement is a natural, everyday part of their thinking—so much so that many of the choices they make each day are made with achievement in mind.

What's important to note about this is that success people think of achievement not just in regard to their major accomplishments; they also have the same achievement mindset when it comes to the smaller things they do each day. That's because success people see themselves as being personally responsible for everything they do; they take responsibility for doing their best in all of their actions.

So, to success people, 'achievement' is the expected outcome of both their large endeavors and also the minor steps they take throughout the day. In everything they do, their expectation and their intention is to create a 'positive result'—which is what *achievement* really means.

Being aware of your achievements—large and small—is especially important for the benefit it brings to your sense of well-being. It is one of the ways in which your choices are self-evaluated and graded; it allows you to correct things that aren't working and to be aware of the things you're doing right, take positive pride in doing them, and continue to do more of the same.

* * *

Why **achievement** *matters:*

A mindset of achievement is about more than taking major steps or creating great accomplishments. You can be a true achiever even if you live a life that is not made up of headline-making successes. The principal role of achievement in a balanced life is the notion that you are capable of dealing with the details and the opportunities of life—whatever they are—in the most positive and productive way. Doing that leads to a greater sense of well-being and peace of mind—which, ultimately, may be the greatest achievement anyone can have.

* * *

Using *achievement* in a phrase of positive self-talk:

"I am an achiever in every way that counts. I see achievement as an important part of my life, in the biggest and in the smallest ways. I am an achiever, and it shows in everything I do."

90. Wealth

True, intrinsic *wealth* is what you have that makes you glad you're alive. That's why success people measure their wealth by how well their life is working, not just by the balance in their bank account.

When asked to define their wealth, success people might tell you about their family and loved ones, their work and how fulfilling it is, a special creative project they're working on, what their goals are and the progress they're making in reaching them, anything they're doing that helps other people, all of the things they're thankful for, or how beautiful the sunrise was that morning.

That's just some of what *real* wealth is. It doesn't mean material wealth is bad; it isn't. But the people who have their lives in *balance* place money itself low on the list of what wealth means in their lives. That would suggest that the best way to determine your wealth would not begin with totaling up your bank account; it would begin with totaling up your blessings—and reminding yourself why you are here in the first place.

* * *

*Why **wealth** matters:*

A *wealth* mindset, in the form of a belief in prosperity, is a healthy mindset. In this sense, wealth is not the relentless pursuit of material riches, but, rather, the pursuit of adequate means, and enough abundance to share. In the form of spiritual and emotional wealth—perhaps the greatest wealth of all— it can be said that you can never have too much. The summary of a wealth mindset is that instead of fearing scarcity, you choose to actively make abundance a living part of your life.

* * *

Using *wealth* in a phrase of positive self-talk:

"I am wealthy in so many ways. That is because I am blessed in so many ways. Wealth, to me, is the riches in my life that allow me to learn, grow, love, share, and help others live up to their best."

91. Home

As Dorothy says in *The Wonderful Wizard of Oz, "There's no place like home."* No matter how strong or independent a person may be, to the success person, *home* counts.

Home, of course, is the metaphor for your foundation, for your *grounding*. It isn't the location, or the size, or the cost of your home––it's that it's there. It may be your retreat from the negatives and the challenges of the world around you. It may be the place where you dream and plan. Or it may the comfortable, private place where you surround yourself with family or people who believe in you.

Because *home* is on the list of secret words, it gives you the chance to ask yourself four important questions:

1. *How is my grounding?*
2. *How secure do I feel?*
3. *How is my home?*
4. *Is there anything I need to do to improve my home?*

Not every success person always has all of the grounding they need to make their life completely, and at all times, stable. But success people are always aware of the need for that stability, and it is always a part of their thoughts, and a part of their plan.

* * *

*Why **home** matters:*
Creating and maintaining a secure and peaceful place of grounding gives you a respite from the tribulations of the world, and a foundation for your journeys through life. Success can be won alone, and without a space that always awaits to welcome you home. But if you are without a fire in the hearth, you will need to have one in your heart.

* * *

Using **home** in a phrase of positive self-talk:

"I know that being firmly and securely grounded is important to my success in many ways. So I make sure that I make my home a place of love, a place of solace, a place of peace, inspiration, and restoration—and a place of joy, happiness, and great beginnings."

92. Success

Success is what this entire book is about. But as I pointed out in the introductory chapter, we're using an important definition of what *success* means—with a focus on living with *an ongoing sense of well-being.*

You can find out whether you have mastered that kind of success by asking yourself if you're satisfied with your accomplishments, your growth as an individual, and your peace of mind thus far. A good question to ask is *"Overall, how am I doing?"*

You can also measure your success by how you feel when you first wake up in the morning, and how you feel about your life just before you fall asleep at night. The most important thing is that you think about your own success—and what you want to accomplish—as an individual, and then make clear choices about what you're going to do next.

*   *   *

*Why **success** matters:*
Actively focusing on the achievement of success—the attainment of peace of mind and an enduring sense of well-being—is a goal of great worth. A life that lacks clarity on the meaning of success, spends its breath and its energy tilting at windmills—without having a clear direction to follow, or knowing when the battle has been won. When the idea of *'success,'* and what it means to you, is always alive and clear in your mind, *and something on which you focus each day*, you will create more of it in your life.

* * *

Using **success** in a phrase of positive self-talk:

"I choose to be successful—in the most positive, life-enhancing way. I will not wait for life to pass me by. I wake up each new morning and find myself filled with the resolve to live up to the gift this amazing life has given me."

Chapter 11

The Secret Words for
A Life that Works

What are the final secret words that could best describe a life that is working? What would be present in that person's life? We already know it's more than cars and boats and vacations. It's something else, something more meaningful than money or things.

In this chapter, we find the secret words that describe success at a higher level—and the kinds of programs that create that level of success. These words do as much to answer the question, *'What is success?'* as any words we could explore.

As you read each of these final words, the degree they are present in your own life will tell you how well you're doing now, and what you will want to focus on next.

93. Insight

The secret words in this chapter begin with the word *insight*. It is insight that tells each person who practices having it, how well they are doing.

Insight means to 'see within.' It is a gift for some, and an active practice for people who want to understand what's happening in their lives. With insight you see into what's really going on, and understand what is *really* taking place.

Insight is a skill that can be learned. You gain insight when you practice looking for *truth*—for deeper meanings. You learn it by being curious, open-minded, and questioning.

There's a good reason for doing this. Practicing insight can add greatly to your ability to understand yourself, other people, and events. With a deeper understanding of the world around you, you improve your chances of creating the best outcome in any situation.

You cannot have *wisdom*—another of the secret words of success—without having *insight*.

*　*　*

*Why **insight** matters:*
The decisions you make, and the actions you take, are guided by how much knowledge you have. Having *insight* greatly increases the amount of knowledge that is available to you. To operate *without* insight is to deprive yourself of deeper levels of understanding— causing you to rely solely on only the most superficial, and often inaccurate, information to guide you. When you exercise insight—and pay attention to it—you gain knowledge, and your decisions, and your actions, are more intelligent and better informed.

*　*　*

Using *insight* in a phrase of positive self-talk:

"I practice the skill of insight daily. I practice having a deep awareness of people and things. Doing this gives me a greater understanding of the people and the happenings in my life—and improves my ability to deal with any situation."

94. Intuition

Intuition is the ability to sense or know something without consciously knowing how you know it. I have never met a truly successful person who does not have a well-developed sense of intuition.

There is disagreement as to where our intuition comes from. The most likely source of intuited knowledge, if not from the universe itself, is the unconscious mind—the vast, hidden storage centers of the brain. However, it is clear that, regardless of its source, intuition can be developed; it can be 'tuned into,' and it can be improved with practice.

The key to doing that is 'listening within,' and learning to hear what the silence tells you. (Another form of this is in the practice of *mindfulness* in meditation.)

There is a strong correlation between *intuition* and high-level *success*—so much so, in fact, that many people believe intuition itself is one of the key factors in creating it.

* * *

*Why **intuition** matters:*

A well-developed intuition is like having a wise, all-seeing guide that alerts you to secret knowledge that would otherwise be hidden from you. Intuition is part insight, part amygdala function in the brain, and part 'sixth sense'—all working together to feed you subtle information you may need to know. The intuitive message is often so nearly imperceptible it can easily be ignored. But success people don't ignore intuition; they practice listening for it, and recognizing it, so they can master the art of using it.

* * *

Using ***intuition*** in a phrase of positive self-talk:

"I have a strong sense of intuition. I listen for the quiet messages from my subconscious mind that give me unfailing guidance and answers. I have learned to listen to my intuition, and I have learned to follow it."

95. Possibility

Possibility is a remarkable word! It is a word that brings *hope, optimism, promise,* and *positive expectation* with it. Just the thought of 'possibility'—and what it suggests—can add a lift to your day.

When you search for the good, you find the world is *filled* with possibility. The success person recognizes that life is a river with endless bends, and around each of them, possibilities await. Those possibilities live in the form of *ideas, alternatives, insights, breakthroughs, solutions,* and *discoveries*— and the world is filled with them.

This view of life—that the world is ultimately a treasure chest of possibilities— is at the heart of what makes someone a success person. Instead of focusing on the dark and the difficult, success people believe in the dawn and the new revealing—knowing with certainty that there are *always* positive possibilities waiting for them.

In the days of the gold rush, few prospectors happened upon riches by accident; they searched for gold with diligence, knowing it was there waiting to be found. Success people know that *possibilities*, like nuggets of gold, are always there, waiting for those who are willing to seek them out.

Believing in 'possibility' doesn't mean that success people give way to wishful thinking; they don't. They are practical and honest about the challenges they face, but they are also practical and honest about the possibilities and solutions that exist all around them. Success people stand apart from others because they are always mindful of this truth: *possibilities are endless*; they are *always* there.

*   *   *

*Why **possibility** matters:*
People who live *without* a possibility mindset miss the opportunities they could have found—had they only believed in them. Instead of creating the natural energy that comes from finding new solutions and discoveries, people who fail to recognize positive possibilities dissipate what energy

they have, fighting the obstacles and challenges they could have overcome. But the success person does more than just accept the fact that possibilities are an essential ingredient in creating well-being. Knowing that the possibilities are endless, the person with a possibility mindset sees the challenge of the moment as something that *can* be overcome, and positive *possibility* as a certainty of life itself.

*　*　*

Using **possibility** in a phrase of positive self-talk:

"I have a possibility mindset. Each day, I recognize that I have found, and focused on, only a small number of the treasures that are available to me. So I focus often on positive possibilities. I focus on finding them, and on what they can add to my life."

96. Excellence

The pursuit of excellence is one of the most popular and exciting quests in the world of personal growth. *'Excellence'* most commonly represents the high point of achievement in any endeavor, and because of this, seeking excellence is a praiseworthy pursuit.

But for the success people, 'excellence' has a meaning and a value that goes beyond external achievements. To the success people, excellence is more about the development of their *character* than it is about the level of their accomplishment. They are more interested in how well they are progressing as individuals—the level of growth they are reaching on the *inside*—than the heights they are scaling on the *outside*.

It is for this reason that success people are seldom defeated by setbacks. To them, excellence isn't measured by their external successes or failures, but rather by their growth as a result of the experience.

A mindset of excellence also brings with it an important added benefit: focusing on 'internal excellence' creates an attitude of positive expectation—which, in turn, leads to making choices that lead to positive outcomes. So, by working on mastering excellence *within themselves*, success people are creating more successful outcomes—which creates more excellence, overall, in their lives.

* * *

*Why **excellence** matters:*
The person who goes through life *without* a mindset of excellence can lead a life that is acceptable—but seldom a life that is exceptional. For the success person, *excellence* is a guiding principle against which all of their choices and actions can be measured. It is a mindset of 'excellence within' that creates the foundation upon which a life of quality is built.

* * *

Using *excellence* in a phrase of positive self-talk:

"I am a person of excellence. I choose to create excellence in my thoughts, my choices, and my actions. Because I do, I create excellence in my life."

97. Quality

Quality, as the word is used by the most successful, happiest people among us, is not only about someone's home, or their car, or the resort where they vacationed. To the aware people, *quality* is about *life*: quality is a measure of rising to the highest level of their own personal potential.

Creating quality in your life means to take life to a higher level of well-being. Thoughtfully answering the following seven questions will help you define how you feel about the *quality* in your life now.

1. What is the quality of my day?
2. What is the quality of my home?
3. What is the quality of my relationships?
4. What is the quality of my health?
5. What is the quality of my personal growth?
6. What is the quality of my goals?
7. What is the quality of my future?

Having quality in our lives is something we have to practice having, to get it right.

Quality always comes from striving to be better tomorrow than we were yesterday.

* * *

*Why **quality** matters:*
We live in a world where *quantity* relentlessly attempts to surpass *quality* in importance. But the person who fails to recognize the value of quality over quantity will never have a full measure of either. The person who practices having a mindset that pursues quality as a practical ideal will, ultimately, have the edge. The short-term, competitive advantage may be found in a quest for quantity—but well-being and personal fulfillment will always be found in the quest for *quality*.

* * *

Using *quality* in a phrase of positive self-talk:

"I am a person of quality. I look for, find, and create the highest level of quality in every area of my life. I am a quality person, and I live a quality life."

98. Present

In this book, the word *present* means *'in the now.'* It is a word that grounds you in the reality of the moment—where you're *really* at right now. That means that when you're in the present, your mind is not wandering, you're not multi-tasking, and you're not avoiding the moment or whatever you're dealing with right now—you're alive, you're breathing, and you're one hundred percent *aware* of the now.

Success people have vision, and they create their future in their minds, but they also know that to make it happen, you have to be grounded in the present. This is where you are right now. Today counts. This *moment* counts.

Seen in a practical way, the *present* is an amazing gift. It is in recognizing the value of the present that you're able to deal with life as it is, understand who you are and where you are, do what you need to do, and move forward.

* * *

*Why **present** matters:*

Those who have a distracted mindset that keeps them from having a conscious awareness of the present, miss life in real time, as it is actually happening. Without an awareness of the present, you cannot feel it, you cannot sense it, you cannot experience it as it really is—completely in touch with both the richness of the detail and the vastness of your world in that moment. There is always the future to look forward to, and there is always the past to remember. You can do both of those often. But there is only one time in which you can experience the clarity of the present. And that is right now, in this moment.

*　*　*

Using **present** in a phrase of positive self-talk:

"I may dream of the future, but I live in the present. I make sure I am grounded, and living today for today. I love being in the present. This is the 'now' that makes everything work."

99. Mindfulness

The concept and practice of *mindfulness* sits at the crossroads of neuroscience, psychology, and personal growth. Mindfulness is the state of being that is found in meditation, and in other practices, that first deepens the level of your personal *awareness,* and then broadens your understanding. It is the conscious practice of focusing your attention on the present moment, and being completely aware and fully *living* in that moment.

It's easy to understand why the success people like this concept. Being *mindful* sharpens your focus and directs your mind to see the moment with greater clarity. Your thoughts are clear, uncluttered, and more accurate, leading to better decisions and better actions.

At a time when more and more people are going through their days fogging their minds with multi-tasking, bewildered by the massive amount of data and input that is being thrown at them, successful people practice the skill of pausing in midstream, creating focus in the moment, being *mindful*, and regaining control of their thoughts, their direction, and their day.

* * *

*Why **mindfulness** matters:*
People who do not have a mindset of mindfulness are seeing only a fraction of what is before them. Through their lack of conscious awareness, they render themselves less informed, less responsive, and less in control of themselves and their objectives. The more mindful you are, especially in areas in which you wish to excel, the more targeted accuracy you will have in your endeavors. If you want to have all of your mind working for you, and working at its best, an essential track to getting there is a mindset of *mindfulness*.

* * *

Using *mindfulness* in a phrase of positive self-talk:

"Mindfulness is an important part of my life. Each day I practice being mindful, focused, clear, and fully aware within the moment. Practicing mindfulness improves my well-being in a healthy, positive way."

100. Gratitude

Gratitude is so powerful—and so *essential*—that no true success person allows a day to go by without being mindful of it.

If there was one thing you could do, at this moment, to boost your attitude with a single thought, it would be to think of how grateful you are for the blessings you have in your life at this moment.

When you practice doing that often, what follows is a *'cycle of gratitude.'* It starts with being grateful for something, which then opens you up to the possibility of receiving more, which makes you even more grateful for what you have, which prepares you for more—and the positive, upward cycle grows.

Gratitude is such an important ingredient in successful living, because there is a direct relationship between being *grateful* and having a greater sense of *well-being*. People who practice gratitude feel more fortunate, they have a more positive attitude, they overcome hardships—especially emotional hardships—more easily, they get along better with others, they are thankful for today, and they are optimistic about the possibilities of the future. All of those increase with gratitude.

This is because having a mindset of gratitude forms a habit of being mindful of *good*—a daily, personal awareness of the many blessings that come into your life. Instead of looking at the world through the negative lens of self-entitlement or victimhood, your mind is busy focusing on what you *have* instead of what you *lack*.

Choosing to be aware of how grateful you are—and consciously focusing on that gratitude—lifts you up, changes your mental chemistry for the good, gives you an attitude adjustment, and changes the day for the better. Expressing gratitude is something success people become so good at doing, that it is as natural as getting up in the morning——which, to them, usually starts with gratitude.

* * *

*Why **gratitude** matters:*

When you're living in a state of gratitude, life itself is both more *giving*, and more *forgiving*; seeing your world with gratitude, your glass is always half *full*, rather than half empty. In place of over-focusing on the difficulties of life, you see the value and the benefits of being alive—and of being given countless opportunities to grow. There is a great power in thankfulness, but you only bring that power to life when you have a mindset of gratitude—which is one of the things you can do right now, or at any time, to make your life work better.

* * *

Using **gratitude** in a phrase of positive self-talk:

"Every day, for me, is a day of gratitude. I am so thankful to be here, in the classroom of life, with endless opportunities to learn and grow. And one of the things I have learned, is to have gratitude for every day I am here."

101. Peace

The final entry in this book is the word *peace*. It is a fitting way to bring our word journey to a close. Peace is one of the most personally enriching words of all—it is a secret word that holds within it a secret about *you*.

Attaining peace—even for brief moments in time—is both an art and a skill. And it is also one of the most essential forces in your life. The question is not whether there is enough peace in the *world*; the question is whether there is enough peace in your *life*.

Without peace, your brain produces stress-related hormones that diminish your happiness, affect your health, and diminish the quality of your life. *With* peace, your life takes on a tone of well-being. You're not only healthier physically and mentally, but you also have the perspective and the mental and emotional space to think and live in a less stressful, more productive way.

The quest for peace is one of the greatest quests you may ever undertake. No one can live a complete life without it. And those who succeed in finding it, find their true selves within it.

* * *

*Why **peace** matters:*

Without *peace,* there can be no haven of well-being; no sense of serenity, and no clear, calm recognition of the greatest truths of yourself that wait within you. You can *prove* yourself through action and strength and courage and battle—but you will discover the greater essence of yourself during moments of *peace.* That is because it is when the din of the battle is past, and the tumult of the day gives way to quiet and calm, that you regain your connection with that sensibility within you that is the true spirit of who you are. It is that angelic presence, the part of you that loves and cares about you deeply, that comes to say hello, and wish you well—and comes to visit in the quiet, welcoming glow of *peace.* It is within that peace—and only in that peace—that you find the perfect reflection of the real *you.*

* * *

Using *peace* in a phrase of positive self-talk:

"I create deep, life-enriching peace in my life. I know that having peace in my life is very important to me. Every day I create peace in my life, and every day it helps me live a quality life, find myself—and bring out the best of the real me."

Chapter 12

Final Thoughts and Tools You Can Use

Those are the 101 words the success people use most. They are the secret words that have been hidden in plain sight, waiting for us to find them and put them into practice in our own lives.

Wiring The Secret Words Into Your Brain

As we've seen throughout this book, the secret words of success are essential software for your brain. When wired in, they become an operating system for your brain that will direct your thinking in a positive, but practical, way.

To help you wire them in, I'm going to give you some tools I use to help people when I'm working with them. The tools I'm recommending to you here will help you install the new software in the easiest and most lasting way.

1. *"The Secret Words Workbook"*

This workbook was created for people who have read, or are presently reading, the book *The Secret Words of Success,* and who want to identify the key words they should focus on most—and track their progress in an

organized way. You can download *The Secret Words Workbook* (no cost) at:
www.thesecretwordsofsuccess.com/tools

2. Listen to Self-Talk Audio Sessions

The easiest way to install new software in your brain is by listening to it. Because of this, for many years I have written and recorded self-talk audio programs on key subject areas such as self-esteem, weight-loss, finances, health and fitness, career, relationships, taking control of your life, self-esteem for kids, dealing with stress, etc.

The self-talk audio programs are available on a special website so you can listen to them on your phone or listening device. After 30 days, there is a subscription fee, but for the first 30 days you can listen to any of the programs free, as often as you like.

I recommend you try this out. Even listening for the free month will help you begin rewiring your brain with the right kind of self-talk, and it is an excellent way to get started. Listen to the recorded self-talk sessions at:

www.selftalkplus.com

3. *The Secret Words* Wall Poster

This is a printable color wall poster in PDF format. The poster lists all of the secret words of success. Posting it in your home or where you work will keep you mindful of each of the words. Download and print yours (no cost) at:
www.thesecretwordsofsuccess.com/tools

4. *"Six Weeks to Success"* Home Coaching Program

"Six Weeks to Success" is a home coaching program that has helped many people set goals and take action—and have a plan to follow. This is a $149 self-coaching program that I would like you to have as my gift to you. It takes some commitment on your part, but if you take the time to follow the program, you'll get a lot of help from it. Download the *"Six Weeks to Success"* home coaching program (no cost) at:
www.thesecretwordsofsuccess.com/tools

5. Personal Goal-Setting Form

This is the form I use for all of my basic goal-setting. The form is an easy-to-use, one-

page form that lays out each step simply and clearly. This form has been used by thousands of my students, and it is very helpful. You can download the goal-setting form (also at no cost) and make as many copies as you like, at:
www.thesecretwordsofsuccess.com/tools

*   *   *

As you begin to apply the words, you may have a number of old mental programs that don't yet recognize the real (and more successful) you.

But give this some time. The more you change your self-talk—the more your brain receives the new messages—the stronger the new programs will become. In time, the *new* programs will override and replace the old programs, and more of the 'real you' will emerge.

With that in mind, I would recommend one initial, simply-stated goal. It should read something like this: *My goal is: To wire my brain with the very best words, in the very best way.*

Right now, even when you're not thinking about it, you are wiring and rewiring your brain every day. You might as well set a goal to wire it in the best possible way. When you do that, I believe you'll find more of the exceptional person you were born to be. And along with that, you'll find the kind of happiness and well-being that only comes from within.

To live that way, each day, is my wish for you.

Shad Helmstetter
January, 2020

Resources:

The Secret Words of Success Support Tools:
www.thesecretwordsofsuccess.com/tools

To Listen to Self-Talk Audio Sessions:
www.selftalkplus.com

Certified Self-Talk Training:
The Self-Talk Institute
www.selftalkinstitute.com

Life Coach Training:
The Life Coach Institute
www.lifecoachinstitute.com

To Email Shad Helmstetter:
shadhelmstetteroffice@gmail.com

Printed in Great Britain
by Amazon